DATE DUE		
DEC 2 0 1983		
DEC 2 0 1991		
MAR 2 7 1992		
MAY 0 9 1992		
NOV 0 9 1992		
DEC 1 9 1992		
DEC 1 5 1993		

GAYLORD   PRINTED IN U.S.A.

THOREAU AND WHITMAN

A
STUDY
OF THEIR
ESTHETICS

By CHARLES R. METZGER

ARCHON BOOKS
1968

SBN: 208 00691 5
Library of Congress Catalog Card Number: 68-26925
Printed in the United States of America

PREFACE

This present study of the esthetics of Henry Thoreau and Walt Whitman takes its point of departure from an earlier effort regarding the esthetics of Ralph Waldo Emerson and Horatio Greenough, * and represents in one sense an extension of it. I have chosen to add this study of Thoreau's and Whitman's esthetics because I believe that all four writers subscribed in their own ways to closely related versions of the same transcendental tradition. All four of them are Protestant estheticians whose religious views ordered their esthetic convictions. All four were unusually interested in architecture, especially in so far as architecture provided them with clear illustrations of their esthetic positions. With the possible exception of Greenough, all of them are difficult writers, and for similar reasons. They consistently use commonly understood terms giving them highly special and often multiple meanings. For example they frequently discuss art from a religious point of view, using religious terms such as "soul" and "salvation" in developing their arguments.

I chose to consider Emerson and Greenough initially because they came first in time, and because their esthetic theories, however abstruse they appear, are stated directly as theories. I have chosen now to consider Thoreau and Whitman together because even though they are responsible for some very inter-

*Charles R. Metzger, *Emerson and Greenough* (Berkeley and Los Angeles: University of California Press, 1954).

esting theories, they persisted in thinking of themselves as practical men rather than theorists, and their theories are stated for the most part indirectly. I have chosen to consider them after Emerson (and therefore Greenough) because between them they have translated into action what Emerson as theorist called for earlier in his description of the ideal poet. If other poets did "not with sufficient plainness or sufficient profoundness address [themselves] to life, " certainly Thoreau did. If other poets did not "dare . . . chaunt our own times and social circumstances, " certainly Whitman did.

I have chosen to admit persons such as Greenough in the earlier study and Whitman in this present study into the transcendental circle because I am convinced that the epithet transcendentalist indicates more than mere geographical, historical, or social distinction. I believe, as Emerson himself suggested, that the term transcendentalist indicated a special cast of mind, one that has revealed many interesting and rewarding insights into a number of matters, including esthetics. I believe that this transcendental cast of mind is as characteristic of Whitman as it is of Thoreau; even as I have suggested earlier that it is as characteristic of Greenough as it is of Emerson.

Acknowledgments: I should like to thank the editors of the *Annals of Science* and the *Journal of the Society of Architectural Historians* for permission to reprint those sections concerning Thoreau and Whitman which appeared earlier as articles in these journals.

Charles R. Metzger

CONTENTS

THOREAU
AND
WHITMAN

A
STUDY
OF THEIR
ESTHETICS

ONE

A TRANSCENDENTAL
ECONOMIST

Like Emerson the poet and Greenough the sculptor, Henry
Thoreau was a transcendental esthetician. He was a Protestant
communicant with nature; he was a critic and a seer. As a
Protestant communicant he was more extreme than Emerson
or Greenough, being, in his own sense of the terms, more
practical and more mystical than either of them. Like Emerson
he rejected the dominion of the church as an institution and of
the clergy as its agency. "The religion I love, " said Thoreau,
"is very laic. "[1] He objected to formal religion because it was
institutional rather than personal, political rather than poetic.
Like Emerson he complained that the church and the clergy
were not religious enough, and he chose not to join the clergy
for the same reason that Emerson left it: to seek a superior
ministry as a direct communicant in nature.

Like Emerson, Thoreau considered himself a mystic and a
transcendentalist. "The fact is, " he said, "I am a mystic and
a transcendentalist, and a natural philosopher to boot. "[2] He
subscribed to the Emersonian assertion that "all parts of nature belong to one head, as the curls of a maiden's hair. "[3] He
celebrated "Truth, Goodness, Beauty, −[as] those celestial
thrins. "[4] Yet he was less concerned finally with deriving universal principles from nature than with apprehending particulars. "Let me not be in haste, " he said, "to detect the *universal law;* let me see more clearly a particular instance of
it. "[5]

Similarly with respect to salvation Thoreau was less theoretical, more practical than Emerson. He worried less about sal-

vation for American art and more about salvation for the individual artist as practical man. Like Emerson, he sought truth, goodness, and beauty, but as experience, not theory. "I wish to be getting experience,"[6] he said; for he considered the highest truth derivative from experience rather than from faith or reason. "It is when we do not *have* to believe," he argued, "but come into actual contact with Truth, and are related to her in the most direct and intimate way [that] waves of serener life pass over us from time to time."[7] This concern with truth, directly experienced, ordered Thoreau's ideas of worship, of goodness, and of beauty. His ideas on these matters, he insisted, were *merely* those of the practical man who, in seeking direct experience with truth, made this experience the end of all his actions. For he believed that perception of beauty was possible (and only possible) to the practical, to the moral, man. "The perception of beauty," he said, "is a moral test."[8] He saw wisdom and goodness, therefore, less as ends in themselves than as prerequisites to communion with nature and truth, and to the perception of beauty. "The constant inquiry," he said, "which nature puts is 'Are you virtuous? Then you can behold me.' Beauty, fragrance, music, sweetness, and joy of all kinds are for the virtuous."[9] Yet Thoreau's was not the reformer's concern with virtue. "What good I do, in the common sense of the word," he said, "must be aside from my main path and for the most part wholly unintended."[10] He wanted to be virtuous mainly so that he could perceive beauty. To Thoreau of course the highest beauty aside from that incorporate in God's nature lay in the simple, economical, and poetic life of the practical man whose actions were directed toward immediate experiences with the truth, goodness, and beauty present in nature. Such a life constituted Thoreau's idea of salvation, here; "he alone," he said, "is the truly enterprising and practical man who succeeds in maintaining his soul *here*."[11]

Thoreau felt that the main trouble with society was that it had not been set up to allow for the salvation of a truly practical man like himself. Like Emerson he complained that traditions and institutions often supported inaccurate generalizations about life. He described tradition as "a more interrupted and feebler memory,"[12] and he insisted that "no way of thinking or doing, however ancient, can be trusted without proof."[13] He objected even to a man's following "his father's or his mother's or his neighbor's" way of doing anything. "I would have each one be careful to find out and pursue *his own* way,"[14] he said. He went so far as to complain of civilization and its traditions and institutions altogether. "The life of a civilized people," he announced, is "an institution in which the life of the individual is to a great extent absorbed, in order to preserve and protect that of the race."[15] More extreme than either Emerson or Greenough, Thoreau criticized society not in part but *in toto;* yet he appears to have withdrawn from it upon various occasions for the same reasons that Emerson left the ministry and Greenough left the country—namely, that society as he knew it interfered with his plans.

It is easier to withdraw from a church or a country to worship beauty or to practice art than it is to withdraw from society altogether. Even the purist must conduct some business with society however much he disapproves of it. But a limited traffic with society does not rule out criticism entirely: often, as in Thoreau's case, it sharpens it. Thoreau did not, like the anchorite, withdraw wholly from society (even though he agreed with the anchorite that society interferes with salvation of the soul). Instead, he remained in society at least part of the time to argue against it, and from its own Yankee, economical point of view. Such argument was appropriate because Thoreau viewed both the road to salvation and the roadblocks erected on it by society in economical terms.

"Economy," said Thoreau, "is a subject that admits of being treated with levity, but it is not a subject that can be so disposed of."[16] Neither was his main charge that society was uneconomical. It was so, he argued, because it was too complex. Although "we love actions that are simple, which are all poetic," he said, our life in society "is frittered away in detail."[17] "As for the complex ways of living," he added, "I love them not, however much I practice them."[18] He disliked them because of the irrelevant demands which they made upon time better devoted to the "proper pursuit" of salvation, here.

Although Thoreau's critique of society was economically oriented, the currency by which he totaled its accounts differed from his neighbor's. To Thoreau cost was counted not

in dollars but in the "amount of . . . life which is required to
be exchanged for [a thing], immediately or in the long run."[19]
Yet the chief problem of Thoreau's economy, as of anybody
else's, was getting a living. This problem was made uncom-
monly difficult by Thoreau's insistence that he should get his
"living honestly, with freedom left for proper pursuits"[20]—
which is to say for salvation. He found the commoner ways
of getting a living in a dollar economy unsuited to "proper
pursuits." He tried trade, "but found that it would take ten
years to get under way in that, and that then" he would "probably be on [his] way to the devil."[21] He considered farming no
better than trade. It also was too complex. "The farmer," said
Thoreau, "is endeavoring to solve the problem of livelihood
by a formula more complicated than the problem itself. To
get his shoestrings he speculates in herds of cattle."[22] Manufacturing in any organized way he considered downright dis-
honest. "I cannot believe that our factory system is the best
mode by which men get clothing," he said. "The condition of
the operatives is becoming every day more like that of the
English: and it cannot be wondered at, since . . . the principal object is, not that mankind may be well and honestly
clad, but, unquestionably, that the corporation may be en-
riched."[23] Of schoolkeeping he said, "I . . . found that my
expenses were in proportion, or rather out of proportion to
my income, for I was obliged to dress and train, not to say
think and believe, accordingly, and I lost my time into the
bargaining. As I did not teach for the good of my fellow-men,
but simply for a livelihood, this was a failure."[24] Thoreau
was doubtful anyway of the value of institutional instruction.
The occupation of teaching seemed to dissipate not only the
teacher's integrity and time, but the student's as well. Even
economy was taught in an impertinent manner. "The poor student," he said, "studies and is taught only political economy,
while the economy of living which is synonymous with philosophy is not even sincerely professed in our colleges."[25]

The trouble with teaching was that both the instructor and the
student were too far removed from nature and, hence, truth.
"The lover of books and systems," said Thoreau, "knows nature [and hence truth] chiefly at second hand."[26] This removal
from nature, from truth, from the possibility of salvation here,

characterized not only the profession of teaching but life generally in society and constituted a threat to a man's moral and intellectual health. "How important, " said Thoreau, "is a constant intercourse with nature and the contemplation of natural phenomena to the preservation of moral and intellectual health. "[27] "But in society you will not find health, but [only] in nature. . . . Society is always diseased, and the best is the sickest. "[28]

Unable in society to get a living that allowed him to maintain his health and to transact the business of salvation, Thoreau tried removing from it. "I turned my face more exclusively than ever to the woods, " he said. "I determined to go into business at once [the business of salvation] and not wait to acquire the usual capital, using such slender means as I had already got. "[29] Applying the ethics of a dollar economy to his own purpose, Thoreau announced that his intention "in going to Walden Pond was not to live cheaply nor to live dearly there, but to transact some private business with the fewest obstacles; to be hindered from accomplishing which for the want of a little common sense, a little enterprise and business talent, appeared not so sad as foolish. " "I have always endeavored to acquire strict business habits, " he said; "they are indispensable to every man. "[30] Like any other businessman Thoreau chose Walden as the site of his enterprise because of its convenient location—in nature. "I seek acquaintance with Nature, " he announced, "—to know her moods and manners. "[31]

Thoreau's concern with economy went considerably beyond a rationale for rejecting society—for setting up to do business in nature; it involved considerably more than a rather witty critique of an acquisitive way of life. Economy was the principal concept ordering both Thoreau's ethics and his esthetics. Only through exercise of the strictest economy did he consider salvation, here, possible for a practical man like himself. Yet in adopting economy as his principal strategy Thoreau betrayed more of the Yankee merchant in himself than he is likely to have admitted. To Thoreau, as to the tradesman, economy involved two coordinated programs of action: (1) the negative, elimination or minimizing of all activity removed from the chosen goal, and (2) the positive, concentration of activity upon attainment of the goal. It was Thoreau's concern with acquiring spiritual wealth as experience in nature rather than material wealth got from society which distinguished him from his more literally acquisitive neighbors. He was a most businesslike mystic; and his rejecting as irrelevant the quest for material wealth was simply the negative manifestation of his enterprise.

Thoreau heavily emphasized this negative economy. Unlike Emerson who usually argued expansively, outflanking the ways of thinking or doing which he opposed, Thoreau argued restrictively, casting these ways out as irrelevant. That he should have argued so is understandable in view of his practical concern with salvation. In his role as prophet Emerson could afford to argue expansively. His insistence that "words are also actions" gave him unlimited freedom to speculate. But Thoreau's concern with "salvation here" limited consideration to what could be accomplished during his own life. As his argument demonstrates, a practical rather than a cosmical concern with salvation leads to a restricted program.

To Thoreau the economical life was a restricted one, characterized by a lowest-common-denominator simplicity from which all things irrelevant to salvation here were canceled out. "I do believe in simplicity, " he said. "It is astonishing as well as sad how many trivial affairs even the wisest man thinks he must attend to in one day . . . [yet] when the mathematician would solve a difficult problem, he first frees the equation of all encumbrances, and reduces it to its simplest terms." "So simplify the problem of life, " he said, "distinguishing the necessary and the real."[32] To this purpose Thoreau retired to Walden, to try his own brand of economy: there to simplify his life, to prepare himself for salvation here by reducing life to its irreducible essentials.

But simplification even in the interest of salvation can be overdone. And after his experiments at Walden, Thoreau remarked, "there are two kinds of simplicity"—two kinds of economy—"one that is akin to foolishness, the other to wisdom."[33] One is the simplicity of the savage; the other is that of the philosopher. "The savage lives simply through ignorance and idleness or laziness, but the philosopher lives simply through wisdom." "The philosopher's style of living, " said Thoreau, "is only outwardly simple, but inwardly complex. The savage's style is both outwardly and inwardly simple."[34]

It is not always easy to tell which kind of simplicity Thoreau subscribed to at any given moment. Speaking of Ruskin's *Seven Lamps of Architecture,* he announced that it "is made of good stuff; but as I remember, there is too much about art in it for me and the Hottentots."[35] Thoreau appears, however, to have identified more often with philosophers than with Hottentots. He may have been thinking of the philosopher's simplicity when he announced that "by simplicity, commonly called poverty, my life is concentrated and so becomes organized, or a κόσμος [cosmos], which before was inorganic and lumpish."[36]

Like most people Thoreau respected the philosopher's organized exercise of "free and absolute thoughts."[37] But as a practical man he made certain characteristic demands. "To be a philosopher," he said, "is not merely to have subtle thoughts, nor even to found a school, but so to love wisdom as to live according to its dictates a life of simplicity, independence, magnanimity, and trust. It is to solve some of the problems of life, not only theoretically, but practically."[38] Thoreau admired the philosopher's intellectual organization only insofar as it contributed to that practical "economy of living" which he considered "synonymous with [true] philosophy."[39] Thus, in reply to the question "to what end do I lead a simple life at all, pray?" he answered, not "that I may teach *others* to simplify their lives," but rather to "lay the most stress forever on that which is most important—imports the most to me."[40] To Thoreau that most important thing was salvation here: by means of economy to achieve communion with nature.

TWO

THE ECONOMIST
AS COMMUNICANT

For Thoreau communion with nature served two related functions: one therapeutic, the other religious and esthetic. He considered nature first of all as a kind of refuge from the poisonous influences of society. "I love Nature partly," he said, "because she is not man, but a retreat from him. None of his institutions control or pervade her."[1] After working four or five days as a surveyor, said Thoreau, "I especially feel the necessity of putting myself in communication with nature again, to recover my tone."[2] He considered this frequent intercourse with nature necessary not only to recuperate from life in society but also to safeguard his morality and his poetic sensitivity. "After having some business dealings with men," he said, "I am occasionally chagrined, and feel as if I had done something wrong, and it is hard to forget the ugly circumstance. I see that such intercourse long continued would make one thoroughly prosaic, hard and coarse. But the longest intercourse with Nature, though in her rudest moods, does not thus harden and make coarse."[3] Thoreau believed, furthermore, that "a man's relation to Nature must come very near to a personal one; he must be conscious of a friendliness in her. . . ." He could not "conceive of any life which deserves the name [without] a certain tender relation to Nature."[4] Such a tender relation to nature was the thing to be sought by the truly practical man above all other things.

But "it is very rare, " said Thoreau,

that I hear one express a strong or imperishable attachment to a particular scenery, or to the whole of nature,—I mean such as will control their whole lives and character. Such [persons] seem to have a
true home in nature, a hearth in the fields and woods, whatever tenement may be burned. The soil and climate is warm to them. They
alone are naturalized, but most [people] are tender and callow crea-
tures that wear a house as their outmost shell and must get their lives
insured when they step abroad from it. They are lathed and plastered
in from all natural influences, and their delicate lives are a long
battle with dyspepsia. The others are fairly rooted in the soil and are
the noblest plants it bears, more hardy and natural than sorrel.[5]

These naturalized persons were the truly practical, the truly
healthy, moral, and poetic; they were such as had achieved
salvation here. This salvation involved an essentially religious
as well as personal connection with nature. The "stillness,
solitude, wildness of nature, " announced Thoreau, "is what
I go out to seek. It is as if I always met in those places some
grand, serene, immortal, infinitely encouraging, though invisible companion, and walked with him. "[6]
    This highly personal connection with nature amounts to a
version of the mystic's direct communion. "Nothing, " said
Thoreau, "so inspires me and excites such serene and prof-
itable thought . . . [as a walk] alone in the distant woods or
fields . . . I come to myself, I . . . feel myself grandly related, and . . . cold and solitude are friends of mine. I suppose that this value, in my case, is equivalent to what others
get by churchgoing and prayer. "[7] Thoreau considered this
communion the most natural and fundamental sort of religious
experience. "I doubt if men ever simply and naturally glorify
God in the ordinary sense, " he said, "but it is remarkable
how sincerely in all ages they glorify nature. "[8]
    While worshipping God in this most fundamental sense, said
Thoreau, the "earth which is spread out like a map around me
is but the lining of my inmost soul exposed. "[9] Such a relation
with nature when experienced continuously over a long period
of time led Thoreau to a feeling of complete correspondence,
to the point almost of blurring the distinctions between nature
and himself. Speaking of nature's seasons, he announced:

These phenomena of the seasons get at last to be—they were at first, of course—simply and plainly phenomena or phases of my life. The seasons and all their changes are in me. . . . Almost I believe the Concord would not rise and overflow its banks again, were I not here. After a while I learn what my moods and seasons are. I would have nothing subtracted. I can imagine nothing added. My moods are thus periodical, not two days in my year alike. The perfect correspondence of Nature to man, so that he is at home in her![10]

This intimate connection of man with nature also charac- terized Thoreau's idea of genius. To Thoreau, as to Emerson, genius was not so much a matter of personal distinction as one of connection with God in nature. Speaking of genius, Tho- reau observed that "men commonly talk as if genius were something proper to an individual. I esteem it but a common privilege, and if one does not enjoy it now, he may congrat- ulate his neighbor that *he* does. There is no place for man- worship. We understand very well a man's relation not to *his* genius, but to the genius."[11] He agreed with Emerson that what passes for personal genius is merely the result of the individ- ual's connection with "the genius." He did not, however, expect as much from persons so connected as Emerson did. Thoreau did not charge genius with solving "the secret enigmas of sci- ence,"[12] with formulating the laws of creation in nature and in art. To Thoreau the individual man as genius was not a hero ded- icated to surpassing the art of the ancients through his formu- lation and application of natural principles. He was merely a man to be congratulated for having achieved communion.

Thoreau did not even believe it necessary for a man to be a genius in order to produce acceptable art. "The man of gen- ius," he said, "may at the same time be, indeed is commonly, an Artist, but the two are not to be confounded."[13] He agreed with Emerson that genius involved both independent thought and original creative activity: "The man of genius," he said, "is an originator, an inspired or demonic man, who produces a perfect work in obedience to laws yet unexplored." But he added that "the artist is he who detects and applies the law from observation of the works of Genius, whether man or nature. The Artisan is he who merely applies the rules which others have detected."[14]

Even though he came close to Emerson's assertion that

"Genius is power; Talent is applicability,"[15] Thoreau made a distinction between the genius and the artist which placed the artist largely within the category of talent. To Emerson it was the artist and the genius who were most closely identified; to Thoreau it was the communicant and the genius. The insights of Emerson's genius as artist were ordered by principles deriving from nature; those of Thoreau's genius as communicant were ordered less by identified principle than by inspiration. "To perceive freshly, with fresh senses," said Thoreau, "is to be inspired. It is only necessary to behold . . . the least fact or phenomena, however familiar, from a point of view a hair's breadth aside from our habitual path or routine, to be overcome, enchanted by its beauty and significance."[16] In this statement Thoreau comes close to Emerson's observation that "Genius seems to consist merely in trueness of sight."[17]

Both Thoreau and Emerson believed that genius extended beyond mere visual acuity—that it involved insight deriving from unusual perspective. But they differed in their views of perspective itself. Emerson believed that the individual genius achieved perspective by his formulation and application of natural principles: not only principles of phenomenal nature but of the mind as well. Thoreau believed that genius achieved perspective directly by way of communion. To achieve this communion and this perspective, he said, "I must walk more with free senses. It is as bad to. *study* stars and clouds as flowers and stones. I must let my senses wander as my thoughts, my eyes see without looking. What I need is not to look at all, but a true sauntering of the eye."[18]

Thoreau believed that the proper approach to nature involved the search "for such inward experience as will make nature significant."[19] He did not rule out the scientist's way of looking at nature, but he did insist upon recognizing the limitations of that approach to nature and to insight. He announced that even

as it is important to consider Nature from the point of view of science, remembering the nomenclature and systems of men . . . so it is equally important often to ignore or forget all that men presume that they know, and take an original and unprejudiced view of Nature, letting her make what impression she will on you. . . . For our science, so called, is always more barren and mixed up with error than our sympathies are.[20]

Natural philosopher that he was, Thoreau's relation to the
science of his day was less cordial than Emerson's. "Nature, "
he said, "is reported not by him who goes forth consciously as
an observer, but in the fullness of life"[21]—not by the scientist
but by the communicant.

Any consideration of Thoreau as a naturalist must take into
account the major reservations which characterized his attitude
toward science. Using a version of Emerson's expansive argument, he complained that the scope of science was too limited.
Speaking of astronomy, he said: "A few good anecdotes is our
science, with a few imposing statements respecting size, and
little or nothing about the stars as they concern man. . . ."[22]
When asked to tell the secretary of the Association for the
Advancement of Science "what branch of science [he] was spe-
cially interested in, " Thoreau had been unable to answer: not,
he explained, from any deficiency on his own part, but because
of the limitations of science and scientists. The traditional
conception of science was not large enough to include what he
was doing. Hence, his declaration that he was "a mystic, a
transcendentalist, and a natural philosopher to boot. " "I should
have told them at once that I was a transcendentalist, " he said.
"That would have been the shortest way of telling them that they
would not understand my explanations."[23]

Thoreau considered the "science" by which his writings are
often judged an inadequate way of knowing. "All science, " he
said, "is only a makeshift, a means to an end which is never
attained . . . the truest description, and that by which another
living man can most readily recognize a flower, is the un-
measured and eloquent one which the sight of it inspires."[24]
"Whatever aid, " cautioned Thoreau, "is to be derived from the
use of a scientific term, we can never begin to see anything
as it is so long as we remember the scientific term which always our ignorance has imposed on it."[25] "Our scientific names
convey a very partial information only. . . . How little I know
of that *arbor vitae,* when I have learned only what science can
tell me! . . . No science does more than arrange what knowledge we have of any class of objects."[26]

Thoreau admitted the value of taxonomical system, its conception of genus and species, in learning to know the plants

around Concord. "We cannot see anything until we are possessed with the idea of it, " he said.

In my botanical rambles I find that first the idea, or image, of a plant occupies my thoughts, though it may at first seem very foreign to this locality, and for some weeks or months I go thinking of it and expecting it unconsciously, and at length, I surely see it, and it is henceforth an actual neighbor of mine. This is the history of my finding a score or more of rare plants which I could name. [27]

But by 1855 Thoreau had got nearly all out of taxonomical system that was useful to him—had learned enough to look beyond nomenclature. By that time "his emphasis had shifted sharply toward an interest in habitat and various other aspects of ecology, and that interest continued and increased until his final illness."[28] In turning away from the identification of genus and species Thoreau argued simply that a science of nomenclature was insufficiently poetic. "Botanies, " he complained, "instead of being the poetry, are the prose of flowers."[29]

The botany of his time did not carry Thoreau far enough into the matter it claimed to deal with. Natural science as taxonomy, he argued, dealt not with the poetry which is in nature, but only with its vocabulary and its grammar. "The artificial system" of classification, he said,

has been very properly called the dictionary, and the natural method, the grammar, of the science of botany by botanists themselves. But are we to have nothing but grammars and dictionaries in this literature? . . . I asked a learned and accurate naturalist to direct me to those works which contain the more particular *popular* account, or biography of particular flowers . . . but he informed me that I had read all, that no one was acquainted with them. . . . [30]

Not finding such biographies as he wanted, Thoreau put together and wrote his own. These "later entries" in his *Journal,* "marked by a definite emphasis on habitat, "[31] exploring the relations of soil, shade, temperature, and even wind currents, to the biographies of individual forms of plant and animal life establish Thoreau as a pioneer ecologist.

To the communicant, ecology provides a much more satisfactory approach to nature than taxonomy. The ecologist in concentrating upon the biography of a particular plant is largely freed from the strictures of order and system. His insight comes from the particular object under study. Thus, Thoreau's study of individual plants squared both with his desire to escape the proscriptions of intellectual system, and with his desire to apprehend what he considered nature's system—one much less arbitrary, much more poetic than the taxonomist's. "In the true natural order," said Thoreau, "the order or system is not insisted on. . . . That which presents itself to us this moment occupies the whole of the present and rests on the topmost point of the sphere [of attention]."[32] Ecology was from Thoreau's point of view simply a more accurate way of looking at nature, one more akin to the communion he called "seeing." It was more accurate because closer to nature, farther from abstract system. "In proportion," he said, "as we get and are near our object, we do without the measured or scientific account. . . ."[33]

As an ecologist Thoreau could commune as well as observe. He could commune for the reason that apprehending the ecology of man in God's nature—nature as it affects man, spiritually, morally, esthetically—encompassed the greater part of his scheme of salvation. Ecology[34] is in this sense the term merely by which modern scientists describe their own more precise approaches to what Thoreau conceived of as natural philosophy, as communion—but without Thoreau's particular religious emphasis. That Thoreau considered this religious emphasis important is suggested by his complaint against conventional "men of science [that] when they pause to contemplate 'the power, wisdom, and goodness' of God, or, as they sometimes call him, 'the Almighty Designer,' [they] speak of him as a total stranger whom it is necessary to treat with the highest consideration. They seem suddenly to have lost their wits."[35] They seemed so to Thoreau because they were scientists merely, not communicants, and, therefore, did not actually know God, nor, from Thoreau's point of view, nature either.

Thoreau believed that the ordinary man of science had particularly damaged his ability to see nature, and to know God, in adopting the rule of objectivity. "I think that the man of science makes [a] mistake," he said, in believing

that you should coolly give your chief attention to the phenomenon which excites you as something independent on you, and not as it is related to you. The important fact is its effect on me . . . [the sci-

entist] thinks that I have no business to see anything else but just what
he defines the rainbow to be. . . . [But] I find that it is not they themselves [i. e. , the rainbows] (with which the men of science deal) that
concern me; the point of interest is somewhere *between* me and them
[the rainbows].[36]

For one thing, said Thoreau, "there is no such thing as pure
objective observation."[37] Even if there were such a thing, he
argued, it would still produce statements that were insufficiently interesting, economical, or poetic. "Your observation
to be interesting, i. e. to be significant," he said, "must be
subjective. The sum of what the writer of whatever class has
to report is simply some human experience, whether he be
poet or philosopher or man of science. The [true] man of science," suggested Thoreau, "is the man most alive whose life
is the greatest event."[38] Such a man of science is like the communicant and poet. He recognizes that "no willful activity whatever whether in writing verse or collecting statistics, will produce true poetry or science."[39]

Thoreau believed that the true scientist, like the true poet,
was the man who could look consciously to nature, as most
people do, and yet see it intuitively as well—he was the student
of nature who was also the inspired man, the communicant.
"The true man of science," said Thoreau, "will know nature
better by his finer organization; he will smell, taste, see,
hear, feel, better than other men. His will be a deeper and
finer experience."[40] For "we do not learn by inference and
deduction and the application of mathematics to philosophy,"
said Thoreau, "but by direct intercourse and sympathy. . . .
We cannot know truth by contrivance and method; the Baconian
system is as false as any other, and with all the helps of
machinery and the arts, the most scientific will still be the
healthiest and friendliest man. . . ."[41] It was not looking merely in terms of intellectual system, but seeing in terms of sympathy, which was Thoreau's principal method as natural philosopher. "How unexplored still," by this method, he remarked,
"are the realms of nature. . . . What we know and have seen
is always an insignificant portion."[42] "How much is written
about Nature as somebody has portrayed her, how little about
Nature as she is, and chiefly concerns us, i. e. how much
prose, how little poetry!"[43] Thoreau assigned these tasks of

exploring Nature as she really is and writing about her poetically to the communicant. He considered it his business, therefore, to experience communion, to seek out God in nature, and
to write poetically about such experience. "My work is writing, "[44] he had announced in his *Journal*.

THREE

THOREAU'S
POETICS

"Every man will be a poet if he can, " said Thoreau; "otherwise a philosopher or a man of science. "[1] Emerson also had announced that "every one would be a poet if his intellectual digestion were perfect. "[2] But it was the genius rather than the poet that Emerson had charged with bringing back art into its proper relationship with nature. "All the particulars of the poet's merit, " he said, "his sweetest rhythms, the subtlest thoughts, the richest images, if you can pass into [the poet's] consciousness . . . would class themselves in the common chemistry of thought, and obey the laws of the cheapest mental combinations. "[3] The genius thinking in terms of these laws was Emerson's champion. Thoreau's champion was the poet. "So far as thinking is concerned, " Thoreau admitted, "surely original thinking is the divinest thing, "[4]—but not merely thinking itself. Thoreau did not subscribe to Emerson's reduction of poesis to intellection. Rather he announced that "poetry is the mysticism of mankind. "[5]

Thoreau was concerned more with the poetic or mythic statement of the facts of nature than with the pronouncement of natural principles themselves. "I would so state facts that they shall be significant, shall be myths or mythologic, "[6] he said. "I love the birds and beasts because they are mythologically in earnest. "[7] The poet who is similarly in earnest, said Thoreau, "will write for his peers alone. He will remember only that he saw truth and beauty from his position. . . ."[8] Thoreau believed the poet's point of view was the most accurate—the one which brought the practical man closest to God in nature. Facts are "seen with the eye of a poet as God sees them, "[9] said Thoreau; and no view could be more accurate than that.

Thoreau believed that the poet, the seer, the man possessing superior vision, combined the highest qualities of both the naturalist and the philosopher. "The collector of [natural] facts, " he said, "possesses a perfect physical organization, the philosopher a perfect intellectual one. One can walk, the other sits: one acts, the other thinks. But the poet in some degree does both; he generalizes the widest deductions of philosophy. "[10] The poet does this, said Thoreau, because he looks upon nature from the larger viewpoint of worship. "All the phenomena of nature need to be seen from the point of view of wonder and awe, "[11] he said. "Men are probably nearer to the essential truth in their superstitions [i.e., in their myths] than in their science. "[12] He insisted that one of the principal dangers to poetic insight was the poet's tendency to slip into a limited, scientific frame of mind. "Every poet, " he said, "has trembled on the verge of science. "[13] Yet "how differently do the poet and the naturalist look at objects!"[14]—how much more limited is the scientist's way of looking compared with the poet's way of seeing. On one occasion he announced flatly that "it is impossible for the same person to see things from the poet's point of view and that of the man of science. "[15]

With philosophy as with science, Thoreau complained of a limited point of view. He believed the "philosopher was in this world as a spectator"[16] merely. "Poetry, " he said, *'implie*ᴄ the whole truth. Philosophy *expresses* a particle of it. "[17] Yet he did not reject philosophy completely any more than he did science. He carefully distinguished between philosophy and what he considered true philosophy, between science and true science, between poetry and true poetry—the true variety of each partaking always of subjective observation, of communion, of transport: with the sum of these, true philosophy, true science, true poetry, incorporate in the experiences of the practical man living in harmony with nature. Only by living in such harmony did Thoreau consider anyone adequately prepared for the practice of true philosophy, true science, or true poetry.

Of the true poet, Thoreau announced: "It is not important that the poet should say some particular thing, but [that he] should speak in harmony with nature. "[18] For the "true poem

is not that which the public read[s]" (any more than the true
poet is that which the public conceives as such); "it is what he
has become through his work."[19] "Our moments of inspiration
are not lost, " said Thoreau, even "though we have no particular poem to show for them: for those experiences have left
an indelible impression, and we are ever and anon reminded
of them. . . . [In them] we are receiving our portion of the
infinite. The art of life. "[20] This is to suggest that the inspirations experienced through communion, and the poetic life
to which such inspirations contribute, constitute the sum and
substance of man's highest art. "There are two classes of men
called poets, " Thoreau said; "the one cultivates life, the other
art. "[21] As Professor Matthiessen has suggested, Thoreau "left
no doubt about which he wanted to be. "[22] He considered the poetic life of the communicant in nature to involve not only the
highest art, but the highest wisdom and the highest morality;
such a life represented both the agency and the end of salvation
here for the truly practical man. "Even the wisest and the best
are apt to use their lives as the occasion to do something other
than live greatly, " said Thoreau. "But we should hang as fondly
over this work as the finishing and embellishment of a poem. "[23]
That Thoreau believed he had lived according to this admonition
is suggested by his announcement in *A Week,* that "My life
hath been the poem I would have writ/ But I could not both live
and live to utter it. "[24] His choice, made early and kept till
the last, to cultivate the poetic life in preference to the poet's
art, leads immediately to the question of what theories regarding art and beauty can be derived from his poetics.

Thoreau assumed that nature's was the highest beauty and
that natural forms constituted the highest art. "There is nothing more handsome than a snowflake or a dewdrop, " he said.
"I may say that the maker of the world exhausts his skill with
each snowflake and dewdrop he sends down . . . in truth they
are the product of *enthusiasm,* the children of an ecstasy finished with the artist's utmost skill. "[25] Thoreau saw the objects
and phenomena everywhere in God's nature as representing
both "artists and subjects, God and Nature!"[26] To him accordingly even the humblest natural object represented the highest
art. "Bring a spray from the wood, " he said, "or a crystal
from the brook, and place it on your mantel, and your house-

hold ornaments will seem plebeian beside its noble fashion
and bearing. '[27] Such assumptions as Thoreau's, when unqual-
ified by active concern with creative art principles, can lead
to what amounts to the contemplative fallacy. They lead to
nonperformance in art: the poet is reduced to nonproductive
contemplation of nature instead of the creation of art forms.

That Thoreau was not involved finally in this fallacy is suggested by the volume of his writings. That he sensed the weakness of his position is suggested by his adding that although the
poet's life is his subject, autobiography is his medium. He did
not choose Emerson's and Greenough's way out of the difficulties inherent in asserting that God's nature is the highest
art: he did not argue that the genius creating new forms in
line with natural principles is emulating God's creative activity
in nature. He argued instead that nature is at once God's art
and his autobiography, and that so is the poet's life.

It becomes apparent that Thoreau's conception of unity was
considerably more limited than either Greenough's or Emerson's. Furthermore, the unity that Thoreau sought in life and
art was expressed implicitly rather than explicitly in his
protest against any but a man's own way of "seeing or doing
things." It was implicit in his idea of communion—in his desire
to live simply, to reduce the problem of living to its simplest
terms. It was implicit finally in his idea of a "true economy
which is synonymous with philosophy"—whereby everything
irrelevant to the attainment of salvation is cast out, and all
else is subordinated to the principal end, the life as poem.

Although Thoreau denied the universal validity of any man-
made principle, he appears to have made economy his own
universal principle. As such, Thoreau's economy is notice-
ably inferior to Emerson's threefold conception of unity. In
recognizing the tendency of the mind to unify, Emerson had
equipped himself to explain the nature of principle itself as
unifying device. In refusing to deal with principle as principle,
Thoreau remained unequipped to judge his own assertion of
economy as principle, and to mark its limitations. Thoreau,
for example, had considerably less success in his efforts to
find confirmation of his universal principle of economy in nature than Emerson did in confirming his threefold assertion
of unity.[28] "Nature, " Thoreau had announced, "will bear the

closest inspection, "[29] as indeed it most certainly will; but not without doing a certain amount of violence to Thoreau's assertion of economy as nature's central characteristic. "Simplicity is the law of nature for men as for flowers, " Thoreau had said. Citing Linnaeus on flowers, he had added: "when the tapestry (corolla) of the nuptial bed (calyx) is excessive, luxuriant, it is unproductive. Linnaeus says, 'Luxuriant flowers are none natural but all monsters, ' and so for the most part abortive, and when *proliferous* 'they but increase the monstrous deformity.'"[30]

In turning to nature from the uneconomical complexities of society, Thoreau probably expected to see there evidence of the economy and simplicity that defined his idea of the poetic life. He was not long in recognizing that nature's economy was not the same as the tradesman's, nor even the poet-naturalist's —that it was in many ways an economy of abundance. "There is none of that kind of economy in Nature that husbands its stock, " he observed, "but she supplies inexhaustible means to her most frugal methods."[31] That he was not entirely satisfied with this prodigality in nature is suggested by his observation that "when Porter apples . . . are ripe, there are also other early apples and pears and plums and melons, etc. Nature by her bounteousness thus disgusts us with a sense of repletion—and uncleanness even."[32] Thoreau had to admit that Nature "has her luxurious and florid style as well as Art, "[33] but he was not happy about it. He suggested almost wistfully that possibly the prodigality of nature was only apparent to the ignorant observer. "Nature would not appear so rich, the profusion so rich, if we knew a use for everything, "[34] he said. Examining a bird's nest, he remarked: "How partial and accidental our economy compared to Nature's. In Nature nothing is wasted. Every decayed leaf and twig and fibre is only the better fitted to serve in some other department, and all at last are gathered in her compost heap."[35] Observing a wooden bridge, he noted that the economic life of the fir tree extends beyond the forest habitat to subsequent functions: "the best material for bridge planking . . . outlasting all other woods!"[36]

As he became more learned in ecology, Thoreau found increasing evidence of an economy of abundance in nature hidden beneath the superficial appearance of prodigality. Even so, he

was capable of throwing up his hands on occasion and exclaim-
ing of Nature that "her motive is not economy but satisfaction."[37] Ultimately Thoreau was concerned less with seeing
economy in nature than with seeing nature economically, from
his own poetic point of view. And what amounts to his theory
of beauty is less dependent upon his observations of economy
in nature than upon his assertion that beauty is a function of
the poetic life.

Thoreau believed it was only possible to see beauty in nature
after having chosen poesis as a way of life. "Nature is beautiful," he said, "only as a place where life is to be lived. It is
not beautiful to him who has not resolved on a beautiful life."[38]
Presumably this poetic way of life was also requisite to the
perception of beauty in man's lesser arts, but Thoreau had relatively little to say of man's art. Of Nature's art, however,
he observed that, "from the right point of view every storm
and every drop in it is a rainbow. Beauty and music are not
mere traits and exceptions. They are the rule and character [of
nature]. It is the exception that we see and hear."[39] Beautiful
"objects," he said elsewhere, "are concealed from our view
not so much because they are out of the course of our visual
ray . . . as because there is no [proper] intention of the mind
and eye toward them. We do not realize how far and widely,
or how near and narrowly we are to look. The greater part of
the phenomena of nature are for this reason concealed to us
all our lives."[40] "Here too," Thoreau added, "as in political
economy, the supply answers the demand. . . . There is just
as much beauty visible to us in the landscape as we are prepared to appreciate, —not a grain more."[41]

Thoreau believed it was unnecessary for a man to cultivate
the arts in order to perceive and to appreciate beauty. All he
had to do was look at nature from the proper point of view.
Early in his *Journal* he reported: "I was inclined to think that
the truest beauty was that which surrounded us but which we
failed to discern, that the forms and colors which adorn our
daily life . . . are our fairest jewelry,"[42] and there is little
evidence that he ever departed from this view. Thoreau pre-
ferred to approach beauty as he approached God: simply, directly, and in nature. He characterized beauty by the same
qualities which he ascribed to the poetic life and to nature,

namely: sincerity, transparency, truth, humility, and above
all these a utility and a luxury beyond the calculation of anything less than a spiritual economy like his own. "Perfect sincerity and transparency, " he said, "make up a great part of
beauty, as in dewdrops, lakes, and diamonds. "[43]

Thoreau's concern with sincerity and transparency led him
to a rustic bias much like Wordsworth's. He insisted, for example, that "the humble or sincere and true is more commonly
rough and weatherbeaten, so that from association we prefer
it. "[44] "The most devoted worshippers of beauty, " he said, are
those by whom "the rude pioneer work of this world has been
done. "[45] This rustic bias brought him close to the dangerous
assumption that picturesque rusticity in nature constitutes the
highest beauty, and that rustic or primitive art is necessarily
man's highest art. The danger here does not lie in assuming
that Nature's art encompasses the highest beauty, but in assuming that the rustic's life and art are superior to all others
simply in being rustic. Thoreau, of course, was no more inclined to celebrate the beauty of the rustic's life and art above
the beauty of nature than he was inclined to celebrate the rustic's poverty over the economy of the philosopher.

Being occupied chiefly with living the beautiful life in nature,
Thoreau had considerably less to say about man's art than
either Emerson or Greenough. As might be expected, however,
he complained that man's art was a poor second to God's nature. Like Emerson and Greenough he complained that man's
art had become divorced from nature. "It has come to this, "
he said, "that the lover of art is one, and the lover of nature
another, though true art is but the expression of our love of
nature. It is monstrous when one cares little about trees but
much about Corinthian columns, and yet this is exceedingly
common. "[46] Thoreau believed man's art inferior to Nature's
for two principal reasons: (1) the experiences got from man's
art are not so rich as those got from nature, and (2) the effects
generally of man's art upon the mind are injurious rather than
sanative. In the first place, he said, "art can never match the
luxury and superfluity of Nature. . . . "[47] In the second place,
he complained, "now [even] the best works of art serve comparatively but to dissipate the mind. . . . "[48] But "the true art
is not merely a sublime consolation and holiday labor which the

gods have given to sickly mortals . . . [but] a human life . . .
not a bald imitation or rival of Nature, but the restored original of which she is the reflection."[49] Compared to "such a work
as this," he said, "whole galleries of Greece and Italy are a
mere mixing of colors and preparatory quarrying of marble."[50]

Only in living life as a work of art could the artist reflect
nature and approach the supreme art of God. Only through the
poetic life—through being at once the poet and the poem—could
man approach the high art of God: not through "bald imitation,"
but by "reflection." Thoreau insisted that the artist cannot
achieve the paradoxical condition of simplicity and wealth characteristic at once of nature, of beauty, and of the poetic life,
by mere imitation. "We are not rich," he said, "without superfluous wealth; but the imitator only copies the superfluity."[51]
Thoreau deplored the irrelevant luxury of imitative art. Like
Emerson and Greenough, he argued for a higher art deriving
from genius. "The art," he said, "which only gilds the surface
and demands merely a superficial polish, without reaching to
the core, is but varnish and filigree. But the work of genius
is rough hewn from the first . . . and has an ingrained polish,
which still appears when fragments are broken off, an essential
quality of its substance. Its beauty is its strength."[52]

The statement above suggests an application of Thoreau's
idea of the philosopher's simplicity to his consideration of art.
He believed that in art, as in the true philosopher's life and as
in nature, true simplicity masks richness. He had said of
nature that "each phase . . . while not invisible, is yet not too
distinct and obtrusive. It is there to be found when we look for
it but not demanding our attention."[53] He said also of high art
that it is at once simple and rich, but rich only to those who
recognize true wealth: "It is the height of art that on first pe-
rusal, plain common sense shall appear; on the second, severe
truth; and on a third, beauty."[54] He believed that "the highest
condition of art is artlessness." "Truth is always paradoxical,"[55] he said.

Thoreau believed that the combined simplicity and richness
of high art, its artlessness, derived from the superior simplicity and richness of the life it described. The richest of all
possible lives being that of the communicant, Thoreau concluded that "he is the richest who has the most use for nature

as the raw material of tropes and symbols with which to describe his life."[56] But with writing as with living, Thoreau considered the tropes and the themes subordinate. "The theme, "
he said, "is nothing, the life is everything. All that interests
the reader is the depth and intensity of the life excited."[57] All
this is to suggest that art is essentially autobiographical, and
that in order for art to be true and beautiful it must proceed
from a true and beautiful life in nature. As has been suggested,
such a conception can lead to nonperformance in the arts. Even
when not pursued to its logical conclusion, it still demands an
autobiographical approach by the artist which can easily limit
him to examining his own personal experience and can separate
him from the experiences recorded by other men thinking.
Hardly anyone will deny that art is unavoidably autobiographical—that it records the artist's efforts, his skills, his experiences, his insights; but most people will insist that autobiography includes indirect as well as direct experiences, intellectual as well as emotional experiences.

What Thoreau had to say about art in general is less satisfactory than what either Emerson or Greenough said. It is
neither so interesting nor so important as his poetics. But
what he had to say specifically about architecture is another
matter and illustrates his own observation that we get some
of our finer insights out of the corner of the eye, while attending to something other than what concerns us chiefly.

FOUR

ARCHITECTURE

AT WALDEN

Thoreau considered Nature's the highest architecture. "The most interesting domes I behold, " he said, "are not those of Oriental temples and palaces, but of the toadstools. "[1] Like Emerson and Greenough, he believed that architectural forms developed from primitive circumstances in nature. Observing the circus tent, he remarked: "the main central curve and wherever it rested on a post, —suggested that the tent was the origin of much of the Oriental architecture, the Arabic perhaps. There was the pagoda in perfection. "[2]

Like Greenough, he complained that in monumental architecture life was subordinated to art rather than conversely. "As for the Pyramids, " said Thoreau, "there is nothing to be wondered at them so much as the fact that so many men could be found degraded enough to spend their lives constructing a tomb for some ambitious booby. . . . Many are concerned about the monuments of the West and East—to know who built them. For my part, I should like to know who in those days did not build them, —who were above trifling. "[3] Like Greenough, he objected to "the American taste for architecture." "Consider the beauty of New York architecture, " he said, "and there is no very material difference between this and Baalbec, —a vulgar adornment of what is vulgar. To what end pray is so much stone hammered? An insane ambition to perpetuate the memory of themselves by the amount of hammered stone they leave. "[4] Thoreau's blindness to the considerable agreement between Greenough and himself may have been due to his "prickly reaction to anything advanced by Emerson, " but it may have been due also to his awareness that Greenough practiced, despite his criticisms of it, the monumental architecture that Thoreau deplored. For Thoreau denied the monumental functions of architecture almost entirely. "It should not be by their architecture but by their abstract thought, " he said, "that a nation should seek to commemorate itself. "[5] Upon this crucial point Thoreau differed from Greenough, who considered "first the organic structure of the works; second their monumental character. "[6]

As poet-communicant Thoreau not only rejected ornament in architecture, in monuments, and in monumental buildings, but he rejected public architecture itself. He believed that only domestic architecture was capable of contributing to the beautiful life in nature. Yet in his concern with domestic architecture he insisted upon attention to its "organic structure" just as Greenough did in regarding all architecture. Thoreau's concern was characteristically more extreme than Greenough's. Greenough had asserted that "the occupants alone can say if they have been well served; time alone can stamp any building as solid. " Thoreau not only announced that architecture is best judged by "the Indweller, " but added that "the indweller is the only builder. "[7] He complained that architecture was too far removed from the lives of ordinary men—that it, like poetry, was too often dominated by a concern with art and not often enough by a concern with life. "What does architecture amount to in the experience of the mass of men?" he asked. "I never in all my walks came across a man engaged in so simple and natural [an] occupation as building his house. "[8]

During his experiment at Walden Pond, Thoreau had opportunity to consider the role of domestic architecture in contributing to the poetic life. He believed, to begin with, that a man's house should not be so costly in time or money as to interfere with his living the good life. "It is possible, " he said, "to invent a house still more convenient and luxurious than we have, which yet all would admit that man could not afford to pay for. "[9] "But, " he said, "if the civilized man's pursuits are no worthier than the savage's, if he is employed the greater part of his life in obtaining gross necessaries and comforts merely, why should he have a better dwelling than the former?"[10] As far as Thoreau was concerned the poetic life came first, and the lesser arts, painting, architecture, carpentry, came after—when they contributed to or reflected such a life.

Thoreau considered the architecture of his cabin at Walden more nearly conducive to the poetic life than that of the buildings in New York, or Concord. At Walden he had reduced domestic architecture very nearly to its extreme simplicity. He had even considered the possibility of living after the manner of Diogenes in a section hands' tool box. "I used to see a large box by the railroad, " he said,

> six feet long by three wide, in which the workmen locked up their tools at night; and it suggested to me that every man who was hard pushed might get him such a one for a dollar, and having bored a few auger holes in it, to admit the air at least, get into it when it rained and at night, and shut the lid and hook it, and so have freedom in his mind, and in his soul be free. . . . Many a man is harrassed to death to pay the rent of a larger and more luxurious box who would not have frozen to death in such a box as this. [11]

Having more than a dollar to spend on his house at Walden, Thoreau chose to style it larger than this sleeping box, to build it to allow more light and air, to be better suited to the life of the writer.

In his *Excursions* and in his *Cape Cod and Miscellanies,* he measured the architectural value of the houses he saw in his travels beyond Concord. He concluded that the New England house was far more economical, more philosophical, than the Canadian house. He wrote:

> As we were passing through Ashburnham, by a new white house which stood at some distance in a field, one passenger exclaimed, so that all in the car could hear him, 'There, there's not so good a house as that in all Canada!' I did not so much wonder at his remark, for there is a neatness, as of circumstances, so to speak, when not rich, about a New England house, as if the proprietor could at least afford to make repairs in the spring, which the Canadian houses do not suggest. Though of stone, they are no better construction than a stone barn would be with us. . . . [12]

He complained particularly of the monumental emphasis in Canadian village architecture: "the only building except the chateau on which money and taste are expended, being the church. "[13]

Although he considered American domestic architecture

superior to Canadian, Thoreau was not blind to the deficiencies
of "modern American houses . . . such as they turn out at
Cambridgeport." "I call them American houses, " he said, "because they are paid for by Americans, and 'put up' by American
carpenters; but they are little removed from lumber . . . the
least interesting kind of driftwood to me. "[14] Like Greenough
he noted the superiority of American naval architecture over
its counterpart ashore. "Perhaps we have reason to be proud
of our naval architecture, " he said,

and need not go to the Greeks, or the Goths, or the Italians, for the
models of our vessels. Sea-captains do not employ a Cambridgeport
carpenter to build their floating houses, and for their houses on shore,
if they must copy any, it would be more agreeable to the imagination
to see one of their vessels turned bottom upward, in the Numidian
fashion. [15]

Probably the most poetic example of domestic architecture
that Thoreau ever found beyond Walden was provided by the
miller at Kaaterskill Falls. "I lodged at the house of a saw-
miller last summer, " wrote Thoreau,

on the Caatskill Mountains, high up as Pine Orchard, in the blueberry
and raspberry region, where the quiet and cleanliness and coolness
seemed to be all one,—which had their ambrosial character. He was
the miller of the Kaaterskill Falls. They were a clean and wholesome
family, inside and out, like their house. The latter was not plastered,
only lathed, and the inner doors were not hung. The house seemed
high-placed, airy, and perfumed, fit to entertain a travelling god. . . .
Could not man be man in such an abode? It was the very light and
atmosphere in which the works of Grecian art were composed, and in
which they rest. [16]

What in addition Thoreau had to say concerning high architecture is so mingled with his criticism of Greenough that it
is necessary to return to the matter of his reaction to the
sculptor and look beyond Professor Matthiessen's remark that
"it was too bad that Thoreau's prickly reaction against anything
proposed by Emerson . . . should have kept him from appre-
ciating that in Greenough he had a natural ally whose mature
thought could have guided his own. "[17] Writing in his journal
on January 11, 1852, [18] Thoreau had said:

R. W. E. showed me yesterday a letter from H. Greenough, the sculptor, on architecture, which he liked very much. Greenough's idea was

to make architectural ornament have a core of truth, a necessity and hence a beauty. All very well, as I told R. W. E., from Greenough's point of view, but only a little better than common dilettantism. I was afraid I should say hard things if I said more. . . .

But as for Greenough's idea, Thoreau added,

I felt as if it was dilettantism, and he was such a reformer in architecture as Channing in social matters. He began at the cornice. It was only how to put a core of truth within the ornaments, that every sugarplum might in fact have an almond or carroway seed in it, and not how the inhabitant, the indweller, might be true and let the ornaments take care of themselves. He seemed to me to lean over the cornice and timidly whisper this half truth to the rude indwellers, who really knew it more interiorly than he. [19]

Thoreau charged, in short, that Greenough was just such a poet as cultivated art rather than life. To this he added his own observation that

what of architectural beauty I now see, I know has gradually grown from within outward, out of the character and necessities of the indweller and builder, without even a thought for mere ornament, but an unconscious nobleness and truthfulness of character and life; and whatever additional beauty of this kind is destined to be produced will be preceded and accompanied, aye, created by a like unconscious beauty of life. [20]

It was Thoreau's reaction to poets that cultivated art rather than life, as much as a prickly reaction to anything suggested by Emerson, which was responsible for his hostile attitude toward Greenough. For even if the two men thought similarly of the architecture of monuments and sailing vessels, [21] such similarities can easily be overstressed and must be matched by recognizing the different attitudes which these men held regarding such things as industry and the machine. Thoreau for his part was mindful of the damage industrialization could do to his scheme for the poetic life. He had complained that the end of manufacturing appeared to be the enrichment of the corporation rather than the consumer's life. He chose the hand-made pail in preference to the machine-made one, even though "they may make equally good pails, and cheaper as well as faster, at the pail factory," because the workman in the pail factory "is turned partly into a machine there himself," i.e., because his relation to his work is not sufficiently poetic. "We admire more, " said Thoreau, "the man who can use an axe or an adze skillfully than him who can merely tend a machine."[22]

Greenough, on the other hand, looked to industry and the machine for suggestions which the laws of the mind applied to manufacture could offer fine art. "if we compare, " he had said, "the form of a newly invented machine with the perfected type of the same instrument, we observe . . . how weight is shaken off where strength is less needed . . . till the straggling and cumbersome machine becomes the compact, effective, and beautiful engine."[23] Similarly with primitive art, Greenough looked for the esthetic principle; Thoreau judged in terms of the poetic life. Greenough observed that "when the savage of the South Sea islands shapes his war club, his first thought is of its use. . . . We admire its effective shape . . . its graceful form and subtle outline . . . [but] we neglect the lesson it might teach."[24] Thoreau saw in the savage's art evidence that even he had lived a rudely poetic life supplemented by crude art forms. "J. Hosmer showed me a pestle which his son had found this summer while plowing, " wrote Thoreau.

It had a rude bird's head, a hawk's or eagle's, the beak and eyes (the latter a mere prominence) serving for a knob or handle. It is affecting, as a work of art by a people who have left so few traces of themselves, a step beyond the common arrowhead and pestle and axe. Something more fanciful, a step beyond pure utility. As long as I find traces of works of convenience merely, however much skill they show, I am not so much affected as when I discover works which evince the exercise of fancy and taste, however rude. It is a great step to find a pestle whose handle is ornamented with a bird's head knob. It brings the maker still nearer to the races which so ornament their umbrella and cane handles. [25]

The preceding passage demonstrates among other things how Thoreau, in refusing to consider principle, failed to see, as Greenough did, the connections between primitive and modern technologies. It becomes apparent in looking beyond these differences in attitude toward manufacture, the machine, toward primitive art, that Thoreau's reactions to what Greenough said are essentially the same as his reactions to Emerson's saying similar things. Thoreau's reactions are those of the practical man in the presence of the theorist. He complained, even as

Greenough admitted, that theory without demonstration was of small value. And he announced accordingly that "when R. W. E. and Greenough have got a few blocks finished and advertized, I will look at them."[26] Thoreau's argument with Emerson and Greenough leads back ultimately to the fact that Emerson and Greenough were unitarian thinkers arguing from principle, while Thoreau was a communicant arguing from direct experience. Thoreau sought to experience beauty rather than to apprehend its principles. Greenough sought unity, order, design, and law or principle—both in nature and in art. He had concluded that in art "there is one truth, even as one God, and . . . organization is his utterance."[27] Like Emerson, he argued from the perception and assertion of divine organization, while Thoreau argued from his own brand of economy.

Thoreau and Greenough both arrived, finally, facing each other at approximately the same position, asserting what amounted to two slightly different versions of the organic principle. The one version was applied to the cultivation of the life; the other to the cultivation of art, with both focused for the moment upon the subject of architecture. It may be well to review briefly Greenough's somewhat less poetic, more consciously theoretical assertion of this organic principle. Greenough's assertion involved the acceptance of two subprinciples: (1) the natural principle of adaptation deriving from the biological sciences, and (2) a principle which approximates closely the less mystical aspects of Thoreau's theory of economy. As an economist, Greenough was concerned with getting at the essential in art, even as Thoreau was concerned with getting at the essential in life. "The aim of the artist," said Greenough, "should be first to seek the essential. . . ."[28]

But Greenough's approach to the essential was not entirely economical in Thoreau's sense. Greenough's approach was initially by way of the principle of adaptation. "The law of adaptation," he said, "is the fundamental law of nature in all structure."[29] In Greenough's version of the organic principle the achievement of economy was secondary to adaptation. "Actual approximation to beauty," he said, "has been [e]ffected *first* by a strict adaptation of forms to functions, *second,* by the gradual elimination of all that is irrelevant or imperti-

nent. "[30] "The aim of the artist, " he said, "should be first to
seek the essential. When the essential has been found, then if
ever will be the time to commence embellishment. " "I will
venture to predict, " he added, "that the essential, when found,
will be complete. "[31]

Greenough's organic principle reveals emphasis upon the
positive or adaptive aspect of economy, with the negative aspect, the elimination, following almost axiomatically. Thoreau's economy reveals emphasis upon the negative aspect of
adaptation: upon eliminating the nonfunctional by way of arriving at the truly economical. Greenough's functionalist assertions and Thoreau's economical assertions come closer to
each other than Thoreau realized.[32] Regarding both literature
and architecture, Thoreau expressed an attitude toward ornament which was almost identical with Greenough's. Speaking
of ornament in literature, he had asked: "Suppose an equal
ado were made about the ornaments of style in literature (as
in architecture), should we be any more likely to attain to a
truly beautiful and forcible style?" To this he answered, "I do
believe that any writer who considered the ornaments, and not
the truth simply, ever succeeded. So are made the *belles
lettres* and *beaux arts* and their professors, which we can do
without. "[33]

Thoreau's economy differed from Greenough's functionalism
primarily in emphasis and application. In furnishing his hut at
Walden, Thoreau was as severe a functionalist as can be found
anywhere. But characteristically he was concerned less with
the adaptation of a single piece of furniture to its intended use
than with judging the contribution of each kind of furnishing to
the conduct of the poetic life. He was concerned less with dis-
covering the most effective and beautiful curtains for his house
than with deciding whether they were necessary at all. Of floor
covering, for example, he announced: "A lady once offered me
a mat, but as I had no room to spare within the house, nor
time to spare within or without to shake it, I declined, pre-
ferring to wipe my feet on the sod before my door. It is best
to avoid the beginning of evil. "[34] "Our furniture, " he said,
"should be as simple as the Arab's or the Indian's. "[35] "Not
that ornamental beauty should be neglected, but at least, let

it first be inward-looking and essential, like the lining of a
shell, of which the inhabitant is unconscious, and not merely
outside garnishing."[36]

Thoreau disagreed most violently with Greenough upon this
matter of adaptation. As has been suggested, he considered
Greenough a dilettante, felt that he cultivated art rather than
life—that he was concerned with adaptation as art-principle
rather than as life-principle. From his own poetic point of
view Thoreau was justified in considering Greenough "a senti-
mental reformer in architecture, beginning his reform at the
cornice, not at the foundation."[37] He was justified not only
because of Greenough's actual connection with monumental
architecture in Washington, but also because Greenough really
did argue his reform in architecture from the consideration
of inappropriate ornament in public and monumental architecture.

As has been mentioned, part of Thoreau's objection to Greenough derived from his own restrictive concern with domestic
architecture, as compared with Greenough's more expansive
concern with public and monumental architecture as well. Still
another part of Thoreau's objection to Greenough derived from
the different way each brought nature into his argument: Greenough bringing in biological nature as authority for principle,
Thoreau bringing in nature metaphorically and poetically as
example. Consider in this latter vein Thoreau's metaphorical
statement about architectural ornament in Walden:

What reasonable man ever supposed that ornaments were something
outward and in the skin merely,—that the tortoise got his spotted shell,
or the shell-fish its mother-o'-pearl tints, by such a contract as the
inhabitants of Broadway their Trinity Church? But a man has no more
to do with the style of architecture of his house than a tortoise with
that of its shell.

By way of clarifying this statement Thoreau added:

What of architectural beauty I now see, I know has gradually grown
from within outward, out of the necessities and character of the indweller, who is the only builder,—out of some unconscious truthfulness, and nobleness, without ever a thought for appearance; and whatever additional beauty of this kind is destined to be produced will be
preceded by a like unconscious beauty of life. [38]

But metaphor, even as principle, has its limitations and

creates its own difficulties. And the difficulty here lies in the fact that man has a great deal to do with determining the style of his house. It would be less poetic but more accurate to say that a man has no more to do with the style of his skeleton than the tortoise with its shell: man's house, as Greenough suggested, is another matter. Thoreau's assertion is essentially poetic and mystical. Such a theory of unconscious adaptation as Thoreau asserted could lead to the celebration of primitive living in huts. He had declared in this vein that "the most interesting dwellings in the country, as the painter knows, are the most unpretending, humble log huts and cottages of the poor"; but he had added that "it is the life of the inhabitants whose shells they are and not any peculiarity in their surface merely which makes them *picturesque.*"[39]

In celebrating the rustic cottage as reflecting the life, the necessities, and the character of its inhabitants, Thoreau approached Greenough's definition of character as "the record of function."[40] But he failed to see that character is also recorded by architectures more complex than that of the rustic poor. Thoreau looked beyond the rustic hut only to suggest that the "citizen's suburban box" might become as interesting as the log hut "when [the citizen's] life shall be as simple and agreeable to the imagination, and there is as little straining after effect in the style of his dwelling."[41] He proposed only that domestic architecture should be improved by improving the indweller's life.

Greenough's less poetic theory of adaptation got more directly to the problem of creating and evaluating art, and appears superior to Thoreau's as practical advice to the artist (in any but Thoreau's sense of the word "practical") because it suggests a broad and reasonable criterion of esthetic judgment. Yet from Thoreau's point of view, accepting Greenough's version of the organic principle was equivalent to abandoning the poetics which ordered and justified his way of life. It is no wonder that Thoreau reacted in a prickly way to the ideas of a man who, in agreeing with him on architecture, threatened his scheme for the poetic life. Thoreau, unlike Greenough, set himself up neither as a theorist nor as a prophet. He was concerned only incidentally with art theory, being a practical man occupied with experiencing the poetic life. From Thoreau's point of view, too great an interest in esthetic principle removed the poet from the life experience and weakened his position as poet, i.e., as communicant and seer. To the extent that Emerson and Greenough were interested in esthetic principle, Thoreau considered them isolated from the necessary and the real. Yet he was scarcely less a transcendental esthetician than either of them. In company with them he was a Protestant, a communicant with nature, a seer, a critic, and a worshipper of beauty. His differences from Emerson and Greenough, though marked, are still differences in emphasis and application. He was not, for example, so much a transcendental theorist as he was a transcendental practitioner. Though he actually wrote considerably less poetry than Emerson, he was more nearly a poet, in Emerson's own sense, than Emerson himself. For it is Thoreau and Whitman together who most exactly represent the two halves of Emerson's ideal poet. They come immediately to mind as positive examples demonstrating the validity of this statement in Emerson's essay: "I look in vain," he said, "for the poet whom I describe. We do not with sufficient plainness or sufficient profoundness address ourselves to life, nor dare we chaunt our own times and social circumstances."[42]

Possibly the most important thing about Thoreau's esthetics is its different emphasis. It is neither so broad as Emerson's nor so concise as Greenough's, yet it is more emphatic. It explores with considerable vigor some of the implications of that part of transcendental art theory which Thoreau considered important—which he considered relevant to his own life. The two things which he emphasized most as poet and practical man were economy and the primacy of the individual life. The importance in esthetics of these two themes is suggested by the fact that, although they were not specifically designed by Thoreau to do so, they suggest major avenues of approach to the problems of creating high art and of judging it.

FIVE

WHITMAN
AS TRANSCENDENTAL
ESTHETICIAN

That Walt Whitman was also a kind of transcendental esthetician is not immediately suggested by his background and
training; he was not born into the traditions of New England
Unitarianism; he did not go to Harvard College. But if, by
these geographical, social, and educational requirements,
Whitman is not strictly a transcendentalist, he comes close
enough on other counts to suggest that considering him one may
prove rewarding.

His most obvious connection with New England transcenden-
talism is by way of his discipleship to Emerson. Such discipleship does not necessarily lead to point-for-point agreement
with the master. As Whitman himself said, "the best part of
Emersonianism is, it breeds the giant that destroys itself. Who
wants to be any man's mere follower? lurks behind every page.
No teacher ever taught that has so provided for his pupil's setting up independently—no truer evolutionist."[1] The better part
of discipleship to Emerson lies in understanding the master,
not in accepting his position without qualification. And it is
in claiming to understand Emerson that Whitman considered
himself a disciple.

Emerson [he said] is not most eminent as poet or artist or teacher, though valuable in all those. He is best as critic, or diagnoser.
Not passion or imagination or warp or weakness, or any pronounced
cause or specialty dominates him. . . . He does not see or take one
side . . . he sees all sides. His final influence is to make his stu-
dents cease to believe in anything, outside of themselves.[2]

Whitman was prepared by his religious background and Prot-

estant temperament to recognize and to welcome likenesses
between Emerson's convictions and his own, and yet to maintain his differences. Although Whitman grew up under the influence of the Dutch and Quaker Pietists in New York[3] and not
the Unitarians of Emerson's New England, there was enough
of the two influences in common to make the ideas of each congenial to the other.[4] Both Emerson and Whitman were extreme
radical Protestants. Like Emerson, Whitman objected to the
dominion of institutions over religious experience. "The time
has certainly come," he said, "to begin to discharge the idea
of religion, in the United States, from mere ecclesiasticism.
. . . "[5] Like most radical Protestants he asserted the doctrine
of the individual priesthood of all believers and accepted as its
corollary the disappearance of a professional clergy. "There
will soon be no more priests," Whitman announced. "Their
work is done. A new order shall arise . . . and every man
shall be his own priest."[6] Like Thoreau he was secular in the
special sense of denying the church as the principal agency of
salvation. He rejected the "mere ecclesiasticism" of the clergy
as too limited. Along with Emerson he chose to extend radical
Protestant religion till it embraced art and the artist; and like
Thoreau he judged art and the artist as these were instrumental
in achieving salvation here.

Like the Quakers and the New England transcendentalists
Whitman turned from institutional guidance to a higher authority, seeking communion with divine authority at its source.
But his approach was less by way of God in nature than by way
of the individual religious conscience—the Quaker's Inner Light.
Along with Thoreau he did consider the "outdoors the best anti-
septic yet."[7] He attributed his improved health after the illness
of 1873 to the fact that he had "been almost two years, off and
on, without drugs and medicines, and daily in the open air. . . .
Never before . . . so close to Nature; never before did she
come so close to me."[8] He recorded in "Specimen Days" a version of Thoreau's mystical communion.[9] But his principal approach to Deity was directly by way of the soul. This concern
with soul per se distinguishes Whitman's brand of communion
from Emerson's, and Thoreau's. Even though Emerson's Unitarianism and Whitman's Pietism represent versions of the
same radical Protestantism, the differences between the

versions are crucially important. These are best seen in terms of a radical Protestant continuum upon which the Unitarian and the Pietist occupy major positions.

Although Emerson enlarged Unitarian doctrine to admit "inspiration and ecstasy,"[10] the original emphasis was upon the individual interpretation of scriptures which left room, as it still does, for a rational interpretation of religious texts by a learned clergy. This rational character of Unitarianism leads, with the gradual abandonment of texts, to a deistical consideration of nature—to a search for knowledge of God, for connection with Deity, via rational study of the designs and principles exhibited in God's nature. A less rational, more enthusiastic version of the deist's attitude is the mystical pantheism of Emerson and Thoreau. Even at its extreme limits, however, the Unitarian religious attitude is predominantly intellectual and metaphysical and relies heavily upon a theological concern with Deity.

The Pietist occupies a position considerably beyond the most mystical extension of Unitarianism. His doctrine of the Inner Light bypasses the critical examination of texts and appeals directly to the individual religious conscience. It teaches, as Whitman says in speaking of Elias Hicks,

the Platonic doctrine that the ideals of character, of justice, of religious action, whenever the highest is at stake, are to be conform'd to no outside doctrine of creeds, Bibles, legislative enactments, conventionalities, or even decorums, but are to follow the inward Deity-planted law of the emotional soul. . . .[11]

The emphasis here is upon the individual conscience, upon religious enthusiasm, upon ecstatic revelation. There is little concern with reason, little need for a learned clergy—little need even to consult God in nature. The Pietist's position is essentially nonintellectual, nonmetaphysical. It assumes the immediate practicality of achieving divine sanction by communion with the individual conscience conceived as representing the soul. Even though, from their positions along this Protestant continuum, the Unitarian metaphysician and the Pietist mystic both argued against the dominion of institutions by appealing to higher authority, their appeals were different. The Pietist got more directly to the final argument from autonomous religious conscience; he not only ruled out institutional

authority, but to a large extent the authority of reason and observation.

In extending the Protestant argument to this final extremity,
the Pietist weakened it. The direct sanction of conscience can
be applied too easily to too many things. When applied consistently to all actions, it exhausts itself. To submit every action
to what may easily become an approving conscience is tanta-
mount to having no conscience at all. That Whitman was aware
of this weakness is suggested by the following long footnote in
his *Democratic Vistas:*

> I am reminded as I write that out of this very conscience, or idea of
> conscience, of intense moral right, and in its name and strain'd con-
> struction, the worst fanaticisms, wars, persecutions, murders, &c.,
> have yet, in all lands, in the past been broach'd, and have come to
> their devilish fruition. Much is to be said—but I may say here, and in
> response, that side by side with the unflagging stimulation of the ele-
> ments of religion and conscience must henceforth move with equal
> sway, science, absolute reason, and the general proportional develop-
> ment of the whole man. . . . Abstract religion, I perceive, is easily
> led astray, ever credulous, and is capable of devouring remorseless,
> like fire and flame. Conscience, too, isolated from all else, and from
> emotional nature, may but attain the beauty and purity of glacial,
> snowy ice. We want for these States, for the general character, a
> cheerful religious fervor, endued with the ever-present modifications
> of human emotions, friendship, benevolence, with a fair field for sci-
> entific enquiry, the right of individual judgment, and always the cool-
> ing influences of material Nature. [12]

Whitman realized that a thoroughgoing Pietist position is too
extreme. Actually he was less radical in his religious and esthetic positions than the Pietism of his background would suggest. He appears somewhere between Elias Hicks and Emerson. As worshippers of beauty whose esthetics derive from
their religious convictions, Emerson, Greenough, Thoreau,
and Whitman may be ranged along an esthetic continuum run-
ning parallel to the above-mentioned Protestant religious continuum. Emerson and Greenough appear, when viewed in this
manner, slightly more radical as estheticians than their religious backgrounds might suggest, arguing finally, even though
in reasoned terms, from the individual conscience deriving
from nature. Whitman appears less radical than his Pietist
background might suggest, admitting to his esthetics the con-

siderations of nature, of metaphysics, [13] and a brand of reasoned argument. Thoreau shows more moderation than might be expected of him, appearing somewhere between Emerson's position and Whitman's: as a rather thoroughgoing pantheist concerned with the salvation of the individual soul, here, but through connection with natural beauty rather than the religious conscience.

Whitman did not ignore phenomenal nature. [14] But because his major emphasis was upon soul, some understanding of Whitman's idea of soul is important. Although he did not define this idea of soul formally, he appears to have conceived of soul in three senses: in an individual sense, a general sense, and a literary sense. In all three his emphasis is primarily ethical rather than metaphysical. He was concerned less with the divine topography of the universe than with the practice of "moral power and ethic sanity." He considered soul in this first, individual, sense roughly equivalent to the individual religious conscience. He saw the surest approach to moral action and hence salvation here by way of communion with this individual religious conscience, through inviting "the outpour [of] God-like suggestion pressing for birth in the soul."[15] "The simple unsophisticated conscience," he said, is "the primary moral element."[16] Although he refined and extended this individual conception of soul, he seems to have derived it from the Pietist doctrine of the Inner Light. Writing of Elias Hicks, he summarized this doctrine as he understood it. Of Hicks, he wrote:

He was very mystical and radical and had much to say of 'the light within.' Very likely this same *inner light* (so dwelt upon by newer men, as by Fox and Barclay at the beginning, and all Friends and deep thinkers since and now), is perhaps only another name for the religious conscience. In my opinion they have all diagnos'd like superior doctors, the real inmost disease of our times, probably any times. [17]

As a communicant Whitman was concerned more, like Hicks, with the inner human conscience, "the inward Deity-planted law of the emotional soul,"[18] than with the laws of nature and the mind. It is for this reason, very likely, that he considered the Unitarianism of Boston a "bloodless religion,"[19] and announced that "it is . . . not consistent with the reality of the soul to admit that there is anything in the known universe more divine [even nature and abstract reason] than men and women."[20] The actual process by which Whitman effected communion with this outpour of "God-like suggestion pressing for birth in the soul" is not entirely clear. There is some likelihood that his method of communing with soul developed from the Pietist's practice of working up a self-induced emotional state known as "enthusiasm"—extending beyond this to a differentiation of the individual conscience—and beyond this even further to a kind of reverential awareness of individual identity. Whitman wrote in *Democratic Vistas:*

> Alone, and identity, and the mood—and the soul emerges, and all statements, churches, sermons, melt away like vapors. Alone, and silent thought and awe, and aspiration—and then the interior consciousness, like a hitherto unseen inscription, in magic ink, beams out its wondrous lines to the sense. Bibles may convey, and priests expound, but it is exclusively for the noiseless operation of one's isolated Self, to enter the pure ether of veneration, reach the divine levels, and commune with the unutterable. [21]

"The Ripeness of Religion," he said, "is doubtless to be looked for in this field of individuality and is a result that no organization or church can ever achieve."[22] "Religion," he said,

> although casually arrested, and, after a fashion, preserv'd in the churches and creeds, does not depend at all upon them, but is a part of *identified soul*, which, when greatest, knows not bibles in the old way, but in new ways— *identified soul*, which can really confront Religion when it extricates itself entirely from the churches, and not before. [23]

Whitman's communion with an awareness of identity (with the identified soul) was superior to the ordinary Pietist's communion with his conscience because it led not only to sanction, which is the most primitive function of communion, but beyond sanction to those insights which are opened up to an individual by his achieving some degree of self-consciousness.[24] It is important to note in passing that Whitman's reverence for the physical body as an aspect of soul, his celebration of sensory experience as contributory to awareness of personal identity, separates him from ascetic pietists like the Shakers and puts him on a side with modern psychologists.

The ultimate extension of this self-consciousness is consciousness of the individual self-as-soul in its context, not only the context of phenomenal nature, but that of all other selves, arriving finally at the consciousness of the self's participation in a generalized, all-inclusive soul. Speaking of this general conception of soul, Whitman announced in his *Democratic Vistas* that to the individual consciousness of the soul the thought of something else must be added,

> *something* before which the magnitude even of democracy, art, literature, &c., dwindles, becomes partial, measurable—*something* that fully satisfies (which those do not). *That something* is the *All*, and the idea of the All, with the accompanying idea of eternity, and of itself, the soul, the soul, buoyant, indestructible, sailing space forever, visiting every region, as a ship at sea.[25]

More particularly, "in respect to absolute soul," Whitman announced that "there is in the possession of such by each single individual, something so transcendent, so incapable of gradations (like life), that to that extent it places all beings on a common level. . . ."[26] He concluded, regarding this All or idea of the All, that

> the climax . . . loftiest range of civilization, rising above all the gorgeous shows and results of wealth, intellect, power, and art, as such—above even theology and religious fervor—is to be its development, from the eternal bases, and the fit expression of *absolute Conscience*, moral soundness, Justice . . . moral conscientiousness, crystalline, without flaw, not Godlike only, entirely human [which] awes and enchants forever.[27]

These two conceptions of soul—as consciousness of the individual self, and as consciousness of the self in relation to the concept of All—suggest immediately Whitman's more compactly stated concern with "independent separatism," "individualism," "personalism," with "the idea of the aggregate," "adhesiveness," "generalization." They also point in the direction of Whitman's idea of democracy—and beyond that to his idea of literature as the soul of democracy. In his *Democratic Vistas* Whitman refers to "this *Soul*—its other name, in these *Vistas*, is *Literature*."[28] In equating soul with literature Whitman not only dignified literature but also prepared himself to argue that literature could be instrumental in attaining salvation here. By expressing through literature the insights he got from communing with the identified soul and with the idea of All, Whitman proposed to help other people who had not achieved communion. Guidance toward such insight is the central function of Whitman's art.

Like Thoreau, Whitman subscribed to an esthetics which supported a practical program for salvation, here. Like Thoreau—like most communicants who have pursued communion beyond the goal of primitive sanction into some new area of insight—Whitman was also a seer; and he brought forth from his communion with soul not only divine sanction, but a vision of democracy and a program by means of it for salvation.

SIX

WHITMAN'S
VISION
OF DEMOCRACY

Walt Whitman's vision of democracy was religious in the same sense as Thoreau's ethics, being concerned practically with salvation here. It was social in extending beyond Thoreau's concern with salvation for the individual self, to a concern with salvation for America, and beyond that for mankind. Like Thoreau, Whitman conceived of salvation in terms of an intimate association with nature as out-of-doors, but for all of American society. As an ideal society, he said, "Democracy most of all affiliates with the open air, is sunny and hardy and sane only with Nature. . . ." "I conceive of no flourishing and heroic elements of Democracy in the United States, or of Democracy maintaining itself at all without the Nature-element forming a main part. . . ."[1] Whitman recommended to all of society that sanative effect of nature which Thoreau prescribed for the individual. He was less concerned, therefore, with individual withdrawal from society to nature than with establishing a more intimate connection between society and nature, and ultimately with soul. He proposed to make withdrawal from society unnecessary. To the extent that Whitman's idea of democracy involved a whole society in close connection with nature, it represents a social extension of Thoreau's economical ethics. Whitman's concern with nature was not, however, so literally pantheistic as Thoreau's, since he accepted the divinity not only of bare natural phenomena, but the divinity even of urban man and his works.[2] Even though Whitman turned occasionally to God in nature for confirmation of his ethics, he appears to have derived his ethics and its confirmation, primarily from his conception of God in man, i.e., of soul.

Fundamental to Whitman's conception of democracy is the idea of the unhampered operation of conscience by free men, subservient only to God and nature. "'The ideal form of human society,'" said Whitman, quoting Canon Kingsley,

'is democracy. A nation—and were it even possible, a whole world—of free men, lifting free foreheads to God and Nature; calling no man master . . . knowing and doing their duties toward the Maker of the universe, and therefore to each other: not from fear, nor calculation of profit or loss, but because they have seen the beauty of righteousness, and trust, and peace, because the law of God is in their hearts.'[3]

To Whitman this overarching law of God in the human heart was not at all incompatible with the lessons of nature. "The greatest lessons of Nature through the universe," he said, "are perhaps the lessons of variety and freedom. . . ."[4] But these lessons, he added, are rarely understood. "It is not only true that most people entirely misunderstand Freedom," said Whitman, "but I sometimes think I have not yet met one person who rightly understands it."[5] To Whitman, freedom and democracy were primarily spiritual rather than political or phenomenal matters, rising above the laws of society, of culture, of religion. "The whole Universe is absolute Law," he said, (including everything in it), and "Freedom" as commonly conceived "only opens entire activity and license *under the law.*"[6] What, therefore, he asked, is freedom properly and spiritually understood? "What is independence?" It is "freedom from all laws or bonds except those of one's own being, controll'd by the universal ones. To lands, to man, to woman, what is there at last to each, but the inherent soul, nativity, idiocracy, free, highest poised, soaring in its own flight, following out itself?"[7]

In asserting his ethics Whitman did not, like Thoreau, deny the value of institutions, of governments. He did place in advance, and above the recognized values of institutions, the value of something else, the something central to his vision. Speaking of this "something else," he said:

After the valuable and well-settled statement of our duties and relations in society is thoroughly conn'd over and exhausted—it remains to bring forward and modify everything else with the idea of that Something a man is (last precious consolation of the drudging poor), standing apart from all else, divine in his own right . . . sole and untouchable by any canons of authority, or any rule derived from precedent, state-safety, the acts of legislatures, or even from what is called religion, modesty, or art.[8]

Central to Whitman's vision of freedom and democracy is the idea, central also to his conception of soul, of the independent identity of the individual conscience, of the right and duty of each individual to be self-consciously autonomous. "The mission of government, henceforth," he said,

in civilized lands, is not repression alone, and not authority alone, not even of law, nor by the favorite standard of the eminent writer [Carlyle], the rule of the best men, the born heroes and captains of the race (as if such ever, or one time out of a hundred, get into the big places, elective or dynastic), but higher than the highest arbitrary rule, to train communities through all their grades, beginning with individuals and ending there again, to rule themselves.[9]

"The purpose of democracy," said Whitman,

is, through many transmigrations . . . to illustrate, at all hazards, this doctrine or theory that man, properly train'd in the sanest, highest freedom, may and must become a law, and a series of laws, unto himself, surrounding and providing for, not only his own personal control, but all his relations to other individuals, and to the state; and that . . . *this,* as matters now stand in our civilized world, is the only scheme worth working from as warranting results like those of Nature's laws, reliable, when once establish'd, to carry on themselves.[10]

The problem of politics and ethics, said Whitman, "is, under permanent law and order, and after preserving cohesion (ensemble-Individuality), at all hazards, to vitalize man's free play of special Personalism. . . ."[11] It was not possible, Whitman believed, to generalize a reliable, self-adjusting, a universal politics or ethics without taking into account the individual identity, the individual soul. "For the treatment of the universal," he said, "in politics, metaphysics, or anything, sooner or later we come down to one single, solitary soul." For

there is, in sanest hours, a consciousness, a thought that rises, independent, lifted out from all else, calm, like the stars, shining eternal. This is the thought of identity—yours for you, whoever you are, as mine for me. Miracle of miracles, beyond statement, most spiritual and vaguest of earth's dreams, yet hardest basic fact, and only entrance to all facts.[12]

Generalizing from this idea of autonomous, individual ethical and political identity, Whitman went on to add that "not that half only, individualism which isolates," is important to the idea of spiritual democracy: "there is another half, which is adhesiveness or love, that fuses, ties and aggregates, making the races comrades, and fraternizing all."[13] His conception of democracy partakes not only of the Pietist doctrine of the autonomous conscience but also the New Testament doctrine of the brotherhood of man. His conception of a democratic aggregate is consistent not only with the Christian doctrine of love (or adhesiveness) but also with his conception of an absolute or collective soul. Whitman believed that only such a conception of the aggregate could be squared with "the most spiritual and vaguest of earth's dreams, yet hardest basic fact." He believed that only such a spiritually and factually ordered conception of the aggregate was congenial to the establishment and maintenance of moral and political laws as reliable and self-regulating as those of phenomenal nature. For it is only "this idea of perfect [or universal] individualism," said Whitman, "that deepest tinges and gives character to the idea of the aggregate."[14] Only such a democratic conception of the aggregate was consistent, at once, with his ideas of the individual and the collective soul and with the lessons of nature—variety and freedom. Whitman believed that individuality, when ordered by respect for the divinely sanctioned individualities of others, was most conducive to the development in society of variety. Near the end of his *Democratic Vistas* he wrote:

As we have shown the New World including in itself the all-leveling aggregate of democracy, we show it also including the all-varied, all-permitting, all-free theorem of individuality, and erecting therefor a lofty and hitherto unoccupied framework or platform, broad enough for all, eligible to every farmer and mechanic—to the female equally with the male—a towering selfhood, not physically perfect only—not satisfied with the mere mind's and learning's store, but religious, possessing the idea of the infinite.[15]

Whitman's social and religious conception of democracy was ideal, spiritual—ordered by his conceptions of freedom, of soul, of universal, spiritual law. It appears to have been the principal consequence of his communion with the Inner Light, and the positive substance of his vision as seer.

But whenever the seer turns away from his ideal vision, he runs into conflict between its afterimage and the spectacle of the real world of objects and events. A seer, such as Whitman, whose vision of the ideal is social as well as religious is particularly susceptible to this hazard. With Whitman as with Emerson, Greenough, and Thoreau, the conflict between this image of the ideal and the spectacle of the real resolved itself into criticism. Hardly less than Emerson, Whitman also was eminent "as a critic or diagnoser." Like Emerson and Greenough he wanted to secure those religious and political freedoms that had already been achieved in America by asserting and establishing similar freedoms in art and esthetics. Like Thoreau, however, he was less confident than Emerson or Greenough of the security even of the political and religious freedoms that had so far been attained. Advancing beyond Emerson and Greenough, he argued not only against foreign influences upon American art but upon American society as well; like Thoreau he criticized not only American art, but American society. Whitman has not often been identified as a critic[16] because his emphasis is primarily upon positive rather than negative aspects of criticism—upon criticism expressed as prophecy, and through the silent defiance of new free forms.

The negative aspect of Whitman's criticism is largely implicit; nevertheless, there remains a considerable body of explicit, negative criticism in Whitman's prose writing. Like Thoreau, for example, he complained that society in America was not simple, and, hence, was uncongenial to proper development of the individual soul. In his *Democratic Vistas* he wrote: "Singleness and normal simplicity and separation, amid this more and more complex, more and more artificialized state of society—how pensively we yearn for them! how we would welcome their return!"[17] Like Thoreau, he complained also that society as currently set up was inimical to soul because of its primary concern with acquiring wealth. In America, he observed, society was more congenial to soul than in Europe only in being less firmly established. "As in Europe," he said,

the wealth of to-day mainly results from and represents, the rapine, murder, outrages, treachery, hoggishness, of hundreds of years ago, and onward, later, so in America, after the same token—(not yet so bad, perhaps, or at any rate not so palpable—we have not existed long enough—but we seem to be doing our best to make it up.)[18]

"Society in these States, " he charged, "is canker'd, crude, superstitious, and rotten. Political, or law-made society is, and private or voluntary society, is also."[19] "It is useless to deny it. Democracy grows rankly in the thickest, noxious, deadliest plants and fruits of all—brings worse and worse invaders—needs newer, larger, stronger, keener compensations and compellers."[20]

Whitman believed that the main trouble with American society, the reason for all the hoggishness, was simply that society lacked an adequate or appropriate soul. "In vain, " he said, "have we annex'd Texas, California, Alaska, and reach north for Canada and south for Cuba. It is as if we were somehow being endow'd with a vast and more and more thoroughly-appointed body, and then left with little or no soul."[21] "America has yet morally and artistically originated nothing. She seems singularly unaware that the models of persons, books, manners, &c. , appropriate for former conditions and for European lands, are but exiles and exotics here."[22] The trouble with American society was not only that it lacked soul, but that what little it had in the way of a conception of identity or soul was inappropriate. "At present, " said Whitman,

these states, in their theology and social standards (of greater importance than their political institutions), are entirely held possession of by foreign lands. We see the sons and daughters of the New World, ignorant of its genius, not yet inaugurating the native, the universal, and the near, still importing the distant, the partial, and the dead. We see London, Paris, Italy—not originals, superb, as where they belong—but second-hand here, where they do not belong.[23]

Like Emerson and Greenough, Whitman saw what he feared most in an increasing rather than a decreasing acceptance by Americans of imported conceptions of culture. It was this idea of culture as generally conceived in America that Whitman criticized most violently. Turning to the word "culture, " he announced: "We find ourselves abruptly in close quarters with the enemy. This word Culture, or what it has come to represent, involves by contrast, our whole theme [i. e., spiritual democracy], and has been, indeed the spur, urging us to engagement."[24] For "as now taught, accepted and carried out, are not the processes of culture rapidly creating a class of supercilious infidels who believe in nothing?"[25] — that is, who lack positive faith? Not to develop, through the exploration of one's conscience and one's consciousness of the self in its universal context, he said, but rather "to prune, gather, trim, conform, and even cram and stuff, and be genteel and proper, is the pressure of our days."[26] "Shall a man," shall an American, asked Whitman, be content under the guidance of such a foreign conception of culture to "lose himself in countless masses of adjustments, and be so shaped with reference to this, that, and the other, that the simply good and healthy and brave parts of him are reduced and clipp'd away, like the bordering of box in a garden?"[27] Unfortunately, said Whitman, "taste, intelligence, and culture (so called) have [always] been against the masses [i.e., inimical to democracy and soul], and remain so. . . ."[28]

Nevertheless, he said, "we pronounce not so much against the principle of culture; we only supervise it, and promulgate along with it, as deep, perhaps a deeper principle."[29] For "the best culture" will not be one of emulation and propriety, but "will always be that of the manly courageous instincts, and loving perceptions, and of self-respect — aiming to form, over this continent, an idiocracy of universalism."[30] Whitman diagnosed as treatment for the condition of American society

a program of culture, drawn out, not for a single class alone . . . but with an eye to practical life, the West, the working men, the facts of farms and jack-planes and engineers. I should demand [he said] of this programme or theory a scope generous enough to include the widest human area.[31]

In short, and to sum up, America . . . must for her purposes, cease to recognize a theory of character grown of feudal aristocracies, or form'd by merely literary standards, or from any ultramarine, full-dress formulas of culture, polish, caste &c., and must sternly promulgate her own new standards. . . .[32]

Then we shall

see that the real interest of this people of ours in the theology, history, poetry, politics, and personal models of the past . . . is not necessarily to mould ourselves or our literature upon them, but to obtain fuller, more definite comparisons, warnings, and the insight to ourselves, our own present, and our own far grander, different, future history, religion, social customs, &c.[33]

As indicated in his criticism of American society's conception of culture, Whitman advanced beyond mere complaint to the framing of a positive program. He did not, like Thoreau, propose to withdraw from society. He saw at least some reason for hope in the political character of American society. In "their politics," he said, "the United States have, in my opinion, with all their faults, already substantially establish'd, for good, on their own native, sound, long-vista'd principles, never to be overturn'd, offering a sure basis for all the rest."[34] He was encouraged also by the vitality of American business and industry. "I hail with joy the oceanic, variegated, intense practical energy, the demand for facts, even the business materialism of the current age, our States," he said. "But woe [he added] to the age or land in which these things, movements, stopping at themselves, do not tend to ideas."[35]

These reasons for hope (the political character of America, its vigor and wealth) suggested to Whitman that the first two stages in the development toward a real and lasting democracy had already been realized in a rough way. But the third and most important stage had scarcely been envisioned. "For the New World, indeed, after two grand stages of preparation-strata, I perceive now a third stage," he said.

> The First stage was the planning and putting on record the political foundation rights of immense masses of all people . . . in the organization of republican, National, State, and municipal governments. . . . The Second stage relates to material prosperity, wealth, produce, labor-saving machines. . . . The Third stage, rising out of the previous ones, to make them all illustrious, I, now, for one, promulge, announcing a native-expression-spirit, getting into form, adult, and through mentality, for these States, self-contain'd, different from others, more expansive, more rich and free, to be evidenced by original authors and poets to come. . . .[36]

Whitman believed that the realization of this third and last stage was absolutely necessary to achieving and securing a democracy at once material and spiritual. "Not only is it not enough," he said,

> that the new blood, new frame of democracy shall be vivified and held together merely by political means, superficial suffrage, legislation, &c., but it is clear to me that, unless it goes deeper, gets at least as firm and as warm a hold on men's hearts, emotions and belief,

as, in their day, feudalism or ecclesiasticism, and inaugurates its own perennial sources, welling from the centre forever, its strength will be defective, its growth doubtful, and its main charm wanting. [37]

Like many of his fellow Americans, Whitman was aware of living in a time of crisis; only he saw the crisis as primarily a cultural one. He saw its major issue that of settling upon a valid conception of soul for America. "Not an ordinary one is this issue," he said. According to its outcome, "the United States are destined either to surmount the gorgeous history of feudalism, or else prove the most tremendous [spiritual and social] failure of all time."[38] Success, he said, would be indicated, as well as secured by "vigorous, yet unsuspected Literatures, perfect personalities and sociologies, original, transcendental, and expressing (what, in highest sense, are not yet expressed at all) democracy and the modern."[39] America, he said, will be unable to "prove itself beyond cavil, until it founds and luxuriantly grows its own forms of art, poems, schools, theology, displacing all that exists, or that has been produced anywhere in the past, under opposite influences."[40] Unfortunately, said Whitman, "the first sign of proportional, native imaginative Soul, and first-class works to match, is (I cannot too often repeat) so far wanting."[41]

Whitman attributed the lack of an emergent, native American culture to the relative immaturity of the country and to its lack of an adequate culture hero. He assumed "democracy to be at present in its embryo condition,"[42] and, therefore, he projected into the future its eventual fruition,[43] which he believed could only come from realizing the need for "a fusion of the States into the only reliable identity, the moral and artistic one."[44] Regarding the preoccupation of Americans with amassing wealth (necessary to sustain democracy but harmful when pursued for its own sake), Whitman predicted that: "Soon it will be fully realized that ostensible wealth and money-making, show luxury &c., imperatively necessitate something beyond—namely, the sane, eternal moral and spiritual-esthetic attributes, elements."[45]

To hasten the development of an appropriate culture (and of an appropriate conception of soul underlying it), Whitman prescribed "a more splendid theology, and . . . ampler and diviner songs"[46]—both of these to be advanced by his champion

of democracy, of culture, and of soul—the divine literatus.
"Our fundamental want to-day in the United States, " he said,

is of a class, and the clear idea of a class, of native authors, literatuses, far different, far higher in grade than any yet known, sac-
erdotal, modern, fit to cope with our occasions, lands, permeating
the whole mass of American mentality, taste, belief, breathing into
it a new breath of life, giving it decision, affecting politics far more
than the popular superficial suffrage . . . accomplishing . . . (what
neither the schools nor the churches and their clergy have hitherto
accomplish'd, and without which the nation will no more stand, per-
manently, soundly, than a house will stand without a substratum) a
religious and moral character beneath the political and productive
and intellectual bases of the States. . . .[47]

This was the problem, not only for America, but for all of
humanity. "View'd today, from a point of view sufficiently
over-arching, " said Whitman, "the problem of humanity all
over the civilized world is social and religious, and is to be
met and treated by literature. The priest departs, the divine
literatus comes. "[48]

SEVEN

THE DIVINE

LITERATUS

Whitman's divine literatus amounted to something like a combination of Carlyle's hero[1] and Emerson's representative
man, i.e., the representative man as hero: not in the role of
superman, but in the role of the full-sized man, appropriate
to Whitman's conception of spiritual democracy, symbol of the
modern and prototype of the truly democratic citizenry to
come. "The pride of the United States," said Whitman, "leaves
the wealth and finesse of the cities, and all returns of com-
merce and agriculture, and all the magnitude of geography or
shows of exterior victory, to enjoy the sight and realization of
full-sized men, or one full-sized man, unconquerable and
simple."[2] The full-sized man, he said, "sees health for himself in being one of the masses. . . ."[3] Being aware of the
identity of his own soul and of its context, he recognizes that
"to be under the general law is great, for that is to correspond
with it."[4] As "liberalist," said Whitman, the full-sized man
"has this advantage over antique or medieval times, that his
doctrine seeks not only to individualize but to universalize."[5]
He seeks not only to be heroic, but to be representatively so.

Whitman's full-sized man suggests an incarnation of Emerson's expansive strategy. He embraces all men and all things.
To him "the idea of political liberty is indispensable."[6] He is
a poet: the "one complete lover . . . of the known universe."[7]
But above all else, he cultivates and preserves his own soul,
his identity. Thus, said Whitman, the literatus, the hero, "the
full man, wisely gathers, culls, absorbs"; he consults other
societies as well as his own, other cultures. Yet he avoids be-

coming "engaged disproportionately in that. . . ."[8] As culture hero, the divine literatus partakes of culture in Whitman's modern, democratic sense. "Book learning is good, " said Whitman, "let none dispense with it, but a man may [be] of great excellence and effect with very little of it . . . " may be, indeed, representative and heroic; for "all book knowledge is important [only] as helping one's personal qualities, and the use and power of a man. "[9] Whitman went so far as to suggest that heroes, "powerful persons and first inventors and poets of the earth never come from the depths of the schools—never. " [10] Such a conception of a culture hero is in line not only with Whitman's lack of formal education, but with the Pietist's assertion of the divine authority of simple conscience in all matters.

Whitman's divine literatus was not only a representative, full-sized man, and a poet, but a theologian as well. As theologian his bias was strictly anti-Calvinist.

> Part of the test of a great literatus [said Whitman] shall be the absence in him of the idea of the covert, the lurid, the maleficent, the devil, the grim estimates inherited from the Puritans, hell, natural depravity, and the like. The great literatus will be known by his cheerful simplicity, his adherence to natural standards, his limitless faith in God, his reverence, and by the absence in him of doubt, ennui, burlesque, persiflage, or any strain'd and temporary fashion. [11]

Whitman's principal complaint against what he called Puritanism was that it was restrictive. "At the risk of being misunderstood, " he said,

> I should dwell on and repeat that a great imaginative *literatus* for America can never be merely good and moral in the conventional method. Puritanism and what radiates from it must always be mention'd by me with respect; then I should say, for this vast and varied Commonwealth, geographically and artistically, the puritanical standards are constipated, narrow, and non-philosophic. [12]

Accordingly, one of the things that Whitman desired of the literatus, one of the things that he considered necessary to realize and to secure his idea of spiritual democracy, was a new and "more splendid theology"[13] to supplant the inappropriate and alien theologies which had been brought to America from European cultures. In line with his expansive strategy and with his reluctance to surrender identity to any less encompassing doctrine than his own, Whitman welcomed science as an aid to the literatus in establishing this new and more appropriate theology. [14] "With science, " he said,

the old theology of the East, long in its dotage begins evidently to die and disappear. But (to my mind) science—and maybe such will prove its principal service—as evidently prepares the way for One indescribably grander—Time's young but perfect offspring—the new theology—heir of the West—lusty and loving and wondrous beautiful. [15]

He added that "for America, and for today, just the same as any day, the supreme and final science is the science of God—what we call science being only its minister—as Democracy is, or shall be also. "[16] Therefore, "in addition to establish'd sciences, " and extending beyond them, Whitman "suggest[ed] a science as it were of healthy average personalism, on original-universal grounds, "[17] a science—i.e., a theology—deriving from his conceptions of soul and of spiritual democracy. This supreme science, this theology which Whitman desired of the divine literatus, involved substantially those ideas regarding soul and spiritual democracy which he documented in his prose writings and expressed in his verse.

Whitman's divine literatus (his full-sized man, his poet, his theologian) is characterized by the same major activities as Emerson's genius: namely, independent thought and creative activity. The independent thought, the insight, characteristic of Whitman's divine literatus is the principal subject here under consideration: it involves Whitman's theology, his vision of democracy, his criticism of society, his diagnosis, his prescription, his prophecy, his esthetics. But independent thought alone is not enough; it requires expression, as theology, as poetry, since it cannot be apprehended by others unless it is given form. Thus the culture hero as independent thinker must inevitably become the culture hero as artist—as the giver of objective form to his independent thoughts. And though Whitman admitted that the hero conceived as the doer of great deeds was (in Thoreau's sense) the primal artist, [18] he insisted, nonetheless, that the divine literatus should produce heroic ideas and heroic forms as well as heroic actions. "A heroic person, " he said, "walks at ease through and out of that custom or precedent or authority that suits him not"—he is an independent thinker and doer. But, added Whitman, "of the traits of the

brotherhood [of heroes] of first-class writers, savans, musi-
cians, inventors and artists, nothing is finer than the silent
defiance advancing from new free forms. . . ." "He is greatest for ever and ever who contributes the greatest original
practical example."[19] Thus, as critic, Whitman had warned
"not to blaat constantly for _Native American_ modes, literature,
etc., and bluster out 'nothing foreign' . . . it would be best
not at all to bother with Arguments against the foreign models
or to help American models—but _just go on supplying American
models._"[20]

Whitman's choice of literature as the medium of his champion is understandable not only because he himself was a literary artist, and because language is the usual medium of theology, but also because language is the most influential, the
most all encompassing of the arts, and admits, even when restricted to belles-lettres, the greatest degree of allusiveness.
Language art, Whitman argued, is the principal and most
ample source, the primary support and evidence, of culture.[21]
"It is not generally realized, but it is true," he said, that

as the genius of Greece, and all the sociology, personality, politics
and religion of those wonderful states, resides in their literature or
esthetics, that what was afterwards the main support of European
chivalry, the feudal, ecclesiastical, dynastic world over there . . .
was its literature, permeating to the very marrow, especially that
major part, its enchanting songs, ballads, poems.[22]

Regarding the influence exerted by language arts, Whitman
observed that "a single new thought, imagination, abstract
principle, even literary style, fit for the time, put in shape
by some great literatus, and projected among mankind, may
duly cause changes, growths, removals, greater that the longest and bloodiest war, or the most stupendous merely political,
dynastic, or commercial overturn."[23] Because of the power
of literature, he said: "Above all previous lands, a great
original literature is surely to become the justification and
reliance (in some respects the sole reliance) of American
democracy."[24] Unfortunately, a class of representative heroes,
of divine literatuses, suitable to the achievement of a great
original literature for democracy was little in evidence. "I
feel with dejection and amazement," said Whitman, "that among
our geniuses and talented writers or speakers, few or none

have yet spoken to this people, created a single image-making work for them, or absorb'd the central spirit and the idiosyncracies which are theirs. . . ."[25]

American poets especially were anything but exemplars of the literatus as culture hero. "The accepted notion of a poet," said Whitman,

> would appear to be a sort of male odalisque, singing or piano-playing a kind of spiced ideas, second-hand reminiscences, or toying late hours at entertainments in rooms stifling with fashionable scent. I think I haven't seen a new-publish'd healthy, bracing, simple lyric in ten years. Not long ago there were verses in each of three fresh monthlies, from leading authors, and in every one the whole central *motif* (perfectly serious) was the melancholiness of a marriageable young woman who didn't get a rich husband, but a poor one![26]

Whitman believed such American poets deficient because they were insufficiently religious, because they lacked a conception of soul appropriate to America. "The fatal defects our singers labor under," he said, "are subordination of spirit and absence of the concrete and of real patriotism."[27] Whitman's conception of the divine literatus is important, therefore, because it clarifies, even as it appears to order, his ideas of the character and function of the ideal poet. He saw this ideal poet as a candid "full-sized man, unconquerable and simple,"—as a seer and a prophet, as an apostle of soul.

Just as Thoreau considered honesty requisite to the poetic life and to high art, so Whitman also insisted that "great poets are to be known by the absence in them of tricks, and by the justification of perfect personal candor. All faults may be forgiven," he said, "of him who has perfect candor."[28] The ideal poet was to be unconquerable as well as candid and simple in being conscious of the identity of his own soul and of its context. Such consciousness would enable the poet to be candid and to rise above the need for deceit or pettiness in defense of any hierarchical distinction. "The greatest poet hardly knows pettiness or triviality," said Whitman. "He is a seer—he is individual—he is complete in himself—the others are as good as he, only he sees it, and they do not."[29] "The American bards," he said, once having perceived the divine identities of their own consciences, as well as the divine identities of all others, "shall be mark'd for generosity and affection, and

for encouraging competitors."[30] The American poet's reaction
to the competition of other poets, of other schools of poets,
past or present, will be better poetry rather than invidious
criticism. "The power to destroy or remould is freely used
by the greatest poet," said Whitman, "but seldom the power of
attack. . . . If he does not expose superior models, and prove
himself by every step he takes, he is not what is wanted."[31]

Whitman believed that the great poet's strategy should be
positive rather than negative, creative rather than destructive,
expansive rather than restrictive. He will be the richest man
and the greatest poet, in short, who encompasses the most.
"The most affluent man," said Whitman, "is he that confronts
all the shows he sees by equivalents out of the stronger wealth
of himself." "The American bard [therefore] shall delineate no
class of persons, nor one or two out of the strata of interest,
nor love most, nor truth most, nor the soul [as commonly con-
ceived] most, nor the body most—and not be for the Eastern
States more than the Western, or the Northern States more
than the Southern,"[32] but be for each and for all. To the greatest poet, "past and present and future are not disjoin'd but
join'd. The greatest poet forms the consistence of what is to
be, from what has been and is."[33]

Yet for all his expansiveness, Whitman's ideal poet was still
an economist akin to Thoreau's. Speaking of the poet's virtue,
prudence, Whitman announced: "It has been thought that the
prudent citizen was the citizen who applied himself to solid
gains, and did well for himself and for his family, and com-
pleted a lawful life without debt or crime. The greatest poet
sees and admits these economies as he sees the economies of
food and sleep, but he has higher notions of prudence."[34] "The
prudence of mere wealth and respectability of the most es-
teemed life appears too faint for the eye to observe at all,
when little and large alike drop quietly aside at the thought of
the prudence suitable for immortality. . . ."[35] The truly prudent man, said Whitman, is concerned (like Thoreau's truly
economical man) with soul.

Only the soul is of itself—all else has reference to what ensues. . . .
The prudence of the greatest poet answers at last the craving and glut
of the soul, puts off nothing, permits no let-up for its own case or

any case, has no particular sabbath or judgment day, divides not the living from the dead, or the righteous from the unrighteous, is satisfied with the present, matches every thought or act with its correlative. . . . [36]

Whitman combines in his conception of the ideal poet the expansive strategy of Emerson's metaphysics with the restrictive strategy of Thoreau's economics: this to an end which is similar, at once, to Thoreau's goal of salvation for the soul by living out the life as a work of art, and to Emerson's goal of salvation for art via recourse to soul. Despite Whitman's concern with salvation, the character of his poet-as-hero is not didactic. "The greatest poet," he said, "does not moralize or make application of morals."[37] Didacticism, after all, is inconsistent with the doctrine of the Inner Light.[38] The poet does not preach, said Whitman, because "he knows the soul," and he knows that "the soul has that measureless pride which consists in never acknowledging any lessons or deductions but its own. But it has [also] sympathy as measureless as its pride, and the one balances the other. . . . "[39] The poet's subjects, said Whitman, are humanity and nature, as these are concretely and phenomenally manifest, but looked upon spiritually, in terms of insights got from communion with soul. Whitman urged poets not to settle in selecting subject matter for high poetry upon anything less than real things. "Poet! beware," he warned, "lest your poems are made in the spirit that comes from the study of pictures of things—and not from the spirit that comes from the contact with real things themselves."[40] Like Thoreau, he insisted upon the poet's deriving his art directly from experience. Like Thoreau also, he insisted that "Nature consists not only in itself, objectively, but at least just as much in subjective reflection, from the person, spirit, age, looking at it, in the midst of it and absorbing it. . . . "[41]

Both Whitman and Thoreau were concerned with nature as the phenomenal context of the individual soul—but Whitman's over-all conception of soul was much more social, less pantheistic in its orientation than Thoreau's, and so accordingly was his conception of poesis. To Thoreau, poesis was roughly equivalent to communion with nature; to Whitman it was more nearly equivalent to prophecy. Whitman's poet, although not

neglecting the celebration of phenomenal nature, had assigned
to him another more important task.

The land and sea, the animals, fishes and birds, the sky of heaven
and the orbs, the forest, mountains and rivers are not small themes
[said Whitman] but folks expect of the poet to indicate more than the
beauty and dignity which always attaches to dumb real objects. . . .
Men and women perceive the beauty well enough—probably as well
as he. . . . They can never be assisted by poets to perceive [beauty
in this sense].[42]

"What the people expect of the great poet" is that he should
"indicate the path between reality and their souls."[43] The poet
can do this through the lyrical expression of his individual,
emotional soul, addressed to all other individual souls and to
the collective soul. "The poetry of the future," said Whitman,
"aims at the free expression of emotion (which means far more
than appears at first) and to arouse and initiate, more than to
define or finish. Like all modern tendencies it has direct or indirect reference continually to the reader, to you or me, to the
central identity of everything, the mighty Ego."[44]

Whitman believed that the mark of the greatest poets is reg-
istered in their concern with this central matter of identity.
Such concern he said connects Shakespeare with George Fox.
"What," he asked, "is poor plain George Fox, compared to
William Shakespeare—to fancy's lord, imagination's heir? Yet
George Fox stands for something too—a thought—the thought
that wakes in silent hours—perhaps the deepest, most eternal
thought latent in the human soul. This is the thought of God,
merged in the thoughts of moral right and the immortality of
identity"[45]—identity which is the "most spiritual and vaguest
of earth's dreams, yet hardest basic fact. . . ."

Whitman believed, in effect, that the expressions of the ideal
poet are both inspiring and inspired, that they constitute the
better part of prophecy. "Prediction," said Whitman, "is a
minor part of prophecy. The great matter is to reveal and outpour the God-like suggestions pressing for birth in the soul."[46]
As a prophet, he said, "the great poet has less a mark'd style,
and is more the channel of thoughts and things without increase
or diminution, and is the free channel of himself."[47] He consults himself, his own soul, his consciousness of the self in
its total spiritual and phenomenal context, and, in a manner at

once poetical and oracular, "without effort and without exposing in the least how it is done . . . brings the spirit of any or all events and passions and scenes and persons some more and some less to bear on your individual character as you hear or read. To do this well, " said Whitman, "is to compete with the laws that pursue and follow time. "[48] It is to produce poetic expression that is at once spiritual and factual, at once personal and universal.

EIGHT

WHITMAN'S
ESTHETICS

Intimately involved in Whitman's poetics is his esthetics. In one sense the entire discussion of Whitman so far has concerned his esthetics. Yet for the very reason that Whitman's esthetics is directly involved in his religious conviction, in his ethics, his esthetics qua esthetics is hard to get at. Because of this difficulty it will be prudent to begin by way of considering Whitman first, in company with Emerson, Greenough, and Thoreau, as an esthetic Protestant.

Like other esthetic Protestants, Whitman objected to the dominion of artistic institutions over art. In a manner characteristic of Emerson, he argued against the strictures of traditional schools of art by expanding the term "school" to the point of encompassing all humanity. Referring to "schools of art—the French school, the German school, the English school, " he said: "What do I care for a school? any school? There's only one school: I don't know what to name it. I belong to that school, whatever its name; the human school, the man and woman school, the heart school. . . ."[1] Along with the various "schools, " Whitman rejected "the conventional themes, " in his *Leaves of Grass*, "the stock ornamentation . . . choice of plots . . . legends . . . myth . . . romance . . . euphemism . . . rhyme." His principal concern was with an original, self-regulating art unhampered by the proscriptions of styles, of rimes or rhetorics, of themes or plots deriving from other times and other occasions than his own. These he considered inimical to original art. "All original art, " he said, quoting Taine, "is self-regulated, and no origi-

nal art can be regulated from without; it carries its own coun-
terpoise, and does not receive it from elsewhere—lives on its
own blood. "[2]

Like others who turned away from the rules and customs of
a proscriptive esthetics, Whitman spoke of nature as superior
to most art. "Nature is rude at first, " he said, "but once begun
never tires. Most works of art tire. "[3] To Whitman, as to
Emerson and Thoreau, nature was beautiful per se ("the only
complete actual poem"), altogether and in each of its parts.
"I do not doubt but the majesty and beauty of the world are
latent in any iota of the world, "[4] he said. Yet Whitman did not
subscribe to literal imitation of phenomenal nature any more
than to imitation of prior art forms. He warned against the
"useless attempt to repeat the material creation, by daguerre-
otyping the exact likeness by mortal, mental means. "[5] "No
prepared picture, no elaborate poem, no after narrative, "
said Whitman, "could be what the thing itself is. "[6] Indeed, "the
true use of the imaginative faculty" is not to imitate natural
objects literally, but to illuminate all the facts and phenomena
of nature, principally human nature, by means of the poet's
awareness of identity or soul. It is "to give ultimate vivifica-
tion to facts, to science, and to common lives, endow them
with the glows and glories and final illustriousness which be-
longs to every real thing and to real things only. "[7] It was by
means of facts (objects and phenomena) represented by words
and considered in terms of identity or soul that Whitman proposed to unite the ideal with the real, the spiritual with the
physical in his art.

"The process," said Whitman, whereby an art, at once factual
and spiritual, is expressed, "so far, is indirect and peculiar,
and though it may be suggested, cannot be defined. "[8] It involves, in a variety of modes, the artist's unhampered approach to his subject. The artist, said Whitman, via

observing, rapport, and with intuition, the shows and forms presented
by Nature, the sensuous luxuriance, the beautiful in living men and
women, the actual play of passions in history and life . . . out of
these, and seizing what is in them, the poet, the esthetic worker, in
any field, by the divine magic of his genius, projects them, their anal-
ogies, by curious removes, indirections, in literature and art. . . .
This is the image-making faculty, coping with the material creation,
and rivaling, almost triumphing over it. [9]

Yet, said Whitman, "to put anywhere before the human eye indoors or out, that which distorts honest shapes, or which creates unearthly beings or places or contingencies, is a nuisance and revolt."[10]

Whitman believed that the problem of the artist was to enliven, to vivify, and to make illustrious, real things, doing so indirectly, without either copying them exactly, or distorting their identities. A working out of this problem is perhaps best demonstrated in the paintings of Whitman's friend Thomas Eakins.[11] In Eakins' portrait of Whitman one can see a portrait which works by indirections. It is very much as Whitman would have art be, and provides a graphic demonstration of what Whitman was after in the larger canvas of his poems. Eakins' is a work which regards not only the physical features of Whitman's person, but also the spiritual facts of Whitman's own conception of identity, of self, of soul. Such presentation of material facts ordered by the supreme fact, the supreme idea of identity, is fundamental to Whitman's esthetics. This idea of identity entered into Whitman's view of nature as well. Not only variety and freedom, he said, but the particular quality of identity or being which attends these, is the lesson of nature. "The quality of *Being*, in the object's self, according to its own central ideal and purpose, and growing therefrom and thereto—is the lesson of Nature"[12]—for men and for art. As has been suggested, Whitman was much less concerned with explaining the development of natural forms, and with deriving from natural principles a guide to a creative art process, than he was with celebrating nature and natural phenomena as the context of the most exalted forms of identity or being—men and women.

One main contrast of the ideas behind every page of my verses, compared with establish'd poems [he said] is their different relative attitude towards God, towards the objective universe, and still more (by reflection, confession, assumption, &c.) the quite changed attitude of the ego, the one chanting or talking, towards himself and towards his fellow-humanity.[13]

Whitman's esthetics, as suggested by his lyric mode, is predicated upon the expression of this self-consciousness of identity or being through appropriate, self-regulating forms. Such a point of departure for a theory of creative activity ap-

pears quite radically different from Emerson's, or Greenough's, or Thoreau's; and yet Whitman also refers to a version
of natural principle—one suggested to him by the quality in
nature of identity or being. Radically different as it appears
in comparison with the attitudes of Emerson, Greenough, and
Thoreau, Whitman's attitude suggests little more than a Pietist-
colored extension of the expressionistic view implicit in Thoreau's assertion that the poet's life is the highest art form.
Like Thoreau, Whitman asserted the validity of communion
with nature for the sake of the individual soul; but he also asserted the validity of art-expression for the sake of America's
collective soul. He was concerned not only with poesis as communion but with poesis as expression and as prophecy. Whitman
was as much a communicant as any of the other transcendentalists. But his emphasis as a communicant was upon the Inner
Light, and that emphasis extended his concern beyond communion itself to the expression as art of the insights deriving
from it.

Whitman saw art properly conceived as an instrument to be
used in realizing his scheme of salvation, and he denied the
value of creative activity and of art solely for their own sake.
He proposed to include in his art "nothing" solely "for beauty's
sake." His scheme of salvation did not permit him to apply to art
itself, at its full strength, his conception of being or identity.
He refused to raise man's art to a level equal to or above that
of man himself. He saw that although the art form as fact has
an autonomous identity of its own, it does not have identity at
the same level as the fully developed man, the literatus, of
whose life it is the mere by-product (even when conceived as
the flower or fruit of that life). Whitman saw in admitting art
and beauty for their own sake the danger of divorcing art from
life. And he called accordingly for a literature not "merely to
copy and reflect existing surfaces, or pander to what is called
taste—not only to amuse, pass away time, celebrate the beautiful, the refined, the past, or exhibit technical, rhythmic, or
grammatical dexterity—but a literature underlying life, religious. . . ."[14]

He was unwilling to accept any attitude toward art which was
contrary to this request. Thus speaking of "art for art's sake, "
he said:

. . . think of it—art for art's sake. Let a man really accept that—let that really be his ruling thought—and he is lost . . . politics for politic's sake, church for church's sake, talk for talk's sake, government for government's sake: state it any way you chose it becomes offensive: it's all out of the same pit. Instead of regarding literature only as a weapon, an instrument, in the service of something larger than itself, it looks upon itself as an end—as a fact to be finally worshipped and adored. [15]

"To me, " he said, "that's all a horrible blasphemy—a bad-smelling apostasy. "[16] "I think of art as something to serve the people [not the state]—the mass: when it fails to do that it's false to its promise. "[17] Of art criticism, therefore, he announced that although

it may be that all works of art are first to be tried by their [strictly] art qualities, their image forming talent, and their dramatic, pictorial, plot-constructing, euphonious and other talents . . . [yet,] whenever claiming to be first-class works, they are to be strictly and sternly tried by their foundation in, and radiation, in the highest sense, and always indirectly, of the ethic principles, and eligibility to free, arouse, dilate. [18]

High art, Whitman believed, must have this ethical character underlying its art qualities in order to escape the eventual excesses, the irrelevancies deriving from a highly developed but precious concern with "art. "

On this particular score Whitman agreed with Charles Baudelaire that "immoderate taste for beauty and art leads men into monstrous excesses. "[19] Concern with the esthetic must be ordered by a higher concern with soul. '"The true question to ask of art, '" said Whitman, quoting the librarian of Congress, '"the true question to ask respecting a book, is, *Has it help'd* any human soul?'"[20] Of his own art, Whitman wrote, "No one will get at my verses who insists upon viewing them as a literary performance, or attempt at such performance [merely], or as aiming mainly toward art or aestheticism.'"[21] As this passage suggests, the major terms by way of which Whitman's esthetics is to be approached are not exclusively terms such as "art, " "beauty, " "poetry, " but also the nonesthetic, religious, social, and political terms already discussed (e.g., "soul, " "self, " "being, " "democracy") that Whitman brought to bear upon esthetic considerations.

Whitman was considerably less concerned with defining esthetic terms than Emerson, Greenough, or Thoreau. What he said about the definitions of such terms as "poetry, " "religion, " "love, " "nature, " appears representative of his attitude toward definition in general:

> Let me not dare, here or anywhere, for my own purposes, to attempt the definition of poetry, nor answer the question what it is. Like Religion, Love, Nature, while those terms are indispensable, and we all give a sufficiently accurate meaning to them, in my opinion no definition that has ever been made sufficiently encloses the name of Poetry. . . .[22]

Whitman appears to have been aware that precise definition might endanger an expansive strategy. Nevertheless, he did give particular values to certain indispensable terms whether he defined them or not, and the problem of getting at the meanings of these terms is one of examining the uses to which the terms have been put in context. For the most part Whitman's uses of such terms as "art" and "beauty" involve those general meanings which he considered sufficiently accurate for common discourse. But Whitman's uses of the terms "aestheticism" and "esthetic" or "esthetik" are another matter, since they suggest by their employment a distinction in Whitman's mind between good esthetics and bad esthetics.

He seems to have used the root term "esthetic" in four somewhat different senses. And though it may be unwise to rely too heavily upon orthographic variations in discriminating one of Whitman's meanings of a term from another, the fact remains that in the five different places where he uses the terms "esthetic" or "esthetik" in either favorable or neutral context he uses the simplified spelling of the term, and in the one place where he uses the term "aestheticism" in a derogatory sense, he retains the more conservative spelling.[23] In the latter case, Whitman uses the term "aestheticism" pretty much in Baumgarten's sense, meaning "criticism of taste, "[24] although that meaning is mingled somewhat with the more common, sufficiently understood meaning of the term, denoting things artistic in general. Referring to "the poet, the esthetic worker in any field, "[25] Whitman uses the term in this second, general, and rather neutral sense. In using the term with reference to the eventual spiritual awakening of American society, Whitman

suggests a third, positive meaning of the term, as associated
with soul or spirituality. He refers thus to "the sane, eternal
moral and spiritual-esthetic attributes of American society."[26]

In the following passage from "Poetry To-Day in America,"
Whitman amplifies his positive meaning of the term "esthetik,"
suggesting finally that it involves not only the artistic and the
spiritual, but the expression of these by appropriate "native
expressers."

Though no *esthetik* worth the present condition or future certainties
of the New World seems to have been outlined in men's minds, or has
been generally called for, or thought needed, I am clear that until the
United States have *just such definite and native expressers in the highest artistic fields* their mere political, geographical, wealth-forming,
and even intellectual eminence . . . will constitute but a more and
more expanded and well appointed body, and perhaps brain, with little
or no soul. [27]

In advancing an esthetics of expression, Whitman comes much
closer to Thoreau than to Emerson or Greenough, who were
more concerned as theorists with "esthetics" in the older
Greek sense (defended by Kant) meaning "the science which
treats of the conditions of sensuous perception."[28] It is not
quite accurate to suggest that Whitman was not concerned with
the perception of beauty, since he clearly was. The fact remains, however, that he was more directly concerned with
apprehending and expressing the thought of identity than with
apprehending and creating beauty per se.

Like Emerson, Greenough, and Thoreau, Whitman subscribed to the Unitarian proposition that art should be simple
and economical, that forms should grow out of their purports
or functions, and that art (i.e., his poems) should suggest a
unity in something like Emerson's cosmic sense of standing in
relation to all things. "The art of art, the glory of expression," said Whitman, "is simplicity."[29] "Of ornaments to a
work nothing outre can be allow'd. . . . Most works are beautiful without ornaments."[30] Speaking of *Leaves of Grass,* in the
1872 Preface, he said, "my form has strictly grown from my
purports and facts and is the analogy of them."[31] "My poems,"
he said, "when complete should be a *unity* in the same sense
that the earth is. . . ."[32] Yet Whitman was not concerned, as
Emerson and Greenough, with unity in the abstract, as a con-

cept applied to the assessment of beauty, or as one of the principal devices of the mind. Although he subscribed to versions of Emerson's simplicity and Greenough's completeness, Whitman did so in a characteristically different way. To a greater extent than Thoreau, even, he concerned himself more with saving the soul here, by means of art and beauty, than with saving art by re-establishing its connection with Deity.

Such esthetic conceptions of unity as may be educed from Whitman's prose writings appear to derive from his prior religious conceptions; and they differ as his religious conceptions differed from the religious conceptions of Emerson, Greenough, and Thoreau. Whitman's conception of soul, of identity, i.e., of unity, was threefold. Underlying this threefold conception of soul is the basic idea of identity or being, in the Hegelian sense. Whitman did not develop this idea to the extent, or in the manner, that Emerson explored his concept of unity or Greenough his concept of completeness. He probably did not do so because he was not functioning primarily in the role of a philosopher, or esthetician, but rather in the role of a prophet—one concerned with promulgating a new theology, a new poetry.

What amounts to Whitman's religious conception of unity centers around his idea of an awareness of personal identity got through communion, and expressed as literature rather than as discursive argument. The basic idea of unity with which Whitman concerned himself as poet and divine literatus involved that particular human identity or being which is capable of self-conscious awareness. "In the center of all" his verse, he said, "and the object of all, stands the Human Being, towards whose heroic and spiritual evolution poems and everything directly or indirectly tend. . . ."[33] Whitman's initial extension of his idea of unity was also ordered by this idea of awareness, and resulted in his asserting that each human being ought to be aware not only of his own identity but of the rightful place of that identity in the context of all other identities, personal and phenomenal. Whitman's extension, by way of a program of action for these two complementary versions of a conception of identity, involved their expression by means of literature. Thus, he had announced in reference to *Leaves of Grass:* "Indeed (I cannot too often reiterate) [it] has mainly been the outcropping of my own emotional and other personal nature—

an attempt, from the first to last, to put a *Person*, a human
being (myself, in the latter half of the nineteenth century, in
America) freely and truly on record."[34] "As I have lived in fresh
lands, inchoate, and in a revolutionary age, future-founding, I
have felt to *identify* the points of that age, these lands, in my
recitatives, altogether in my own way."[35] In such expression,
he said, whether it be manifest as theology, as art, or as literature, "the spirit and the form are one, and depend far more
on association, *identity* and place, than is supposed."[36] Whitman's development of these ideas of identity suggests, roughly,
social versions of those static, organic, and cosmic orders of
unity which Emerson saw the mind ascribing to things considered beautiful—with this important difference: that all three
orders of unity or identity in Whitman's scheme are given focus
by his idea of soul rather than by a theory of the cosmos or the
mind.

Implicit in Whitman's conception of soul as literature is the
idea that literature is the organic expression of insight got
from realizing the idea of identity and the facts of identity. To
Whitman beauty was the result, properly, of such expression.
To him, not beauty but appropriate expression (which is beautiful per se) is to be sought by the artist. Hence, Whitman's
attitude toward words: "The words of true poems give you more
than poems. . . . They do not seek beauty—they are sought,
Forever touching them, or close upon them follows beauty."[37]
This amounts to saying that words have greater, albeit more
nebulous, meaning out of context than in, and leads to Whitman's assertion that the thing which orders words, which fixes
at one instance in language some of the meanings of them is
"the purport" of the author. What is responsible for the selec-
tion of a particular word is the experience, the facts of the
author's acquaintance with language and with the things that
suggest language.

By way of pursuing this matter further it will be well to review in some detail Whitman's assertion that "My form has
strictly grown from my purports and facts and is the analogy
of them."[38] As has been suggested, Whitman's purport as an
artist was twofold. In the first place it was to promulgate the
idea of identity by means of art addressed to the soul. Such art
was to operate by indirections, i.e., by demonstration rather

than by assertion. This demonstration was Whitman's second
purport, and involved recording the identity of an exemplary
person, himself, his facts (phenomenal, emotional, conceptual)·
fully and truly.

That the form of Whitman's art actually did grow from his
purports and facts can hardly be denied. It is possible to argue
by way of weakening Whitman's organic assertion—either in
spreading it too thin or in making it sound commonplace—that
what he has asserted is too true, that it applies to all artists
good or bad and is, therefore, of little value. To this argument
it may be suggested in riposte that applicability to all cases is
the primary character of universal propositions, which are still
treasured by philosophers, scientists, and critics. It may be
suggested as well that the theorems of Euclid are also common-
places.

But the matter at hand is not solely the validity of what Whitman said about the genesis of art forms; it is also how what he
said relates to what Emerson, Greenough, and Thoreau said.
In company with these others, Whitman subscribed to the
growth analogy taken from organic forms in nature. "The
rhyme and uniformity of perfect poems, " he said, "show the
free growth of metrical laws, and bud from them as unerringly
and loosely as lilacs and roses on a bush. . . ."[39] Like these
other theorists, Whitman asserted the necessity in art of organic or dynamic unity. His assertion, however, that forms
grow from the purports and facts of the artist is a more highly
developed version of Emerson's assertion that the mind as-
cribes beauty to those forms which it sees exactly answering
their ends, and it bears a somewhat different emphasis from
Emerson's assertion. It approaches in a different way the
question which immediately follows the general assertion that
art forms ought to grow out of, and in response to, their
functions. That question is: Specifically what functions?

The various assertions representing what is commonly called
the organic principle that have been made by Emerson, Greenough, Thoreau, and Whitman suggest several answers to this
question. Emerson's assertion that "every necessary or organic action pleases the beholder" indicates his primary concern with function in its fine-art (i. e., principally psycho-
logical) sense. Greenough's concern with completeness, with

the sublime as "a mental perception of relations" suggests a similar attention to function in this fine-art sense. His distinction, however, between the monumental and the domestic functions of architecture extends consideration into the area of useful-art function relating more to the satisfaction of creature-type wants than to those exclusively of the mind. Thoreau extends this domestic- or useful-art consideration of function beyond the service of utilitarian or creature functions to include within it a religious function of art. He appears to have considered man's fine-art requirements fulfilled adequately enough by natural forms, leaving to the forms of man's art the fulfillment of those useful-art functions which contribute to the conduct of the life as art. Like Thoreau, Whitman was also concerned with the religious functions of art—only he insisted that art, even Thoreau's life-as-art, should serve religious functions that are social as well as personal, that contribute to the salvation of society as well as that of the individual.

Taken altogether, the several views regarding the functions of art forms that were entertained by Emerson, Greenough, Thoreau, and Whitman suggest that form may be considered in terms of function at four different levels: (1) at the level of the mind, concerning the intellectual operations that create the art object and order appreciation of it; (2) at the level of the art object itself, concerning the relations of the materials and functions of the parts to the functions of the whole; (3) at the level of the artist, concerning the relations of the artist's forms to his view of the world and of the good life for himself; and finally (4) at the level of society, concerning the relations of the artist's entire work to his conception of his role in society. These categories of consideration embrace what might be called the fine art, the useful art, the personal, and the social functions of art forms. Together they encompass in general outline nearly all of the commoner ways of applying the idea of function to the consideration of art.

It is perhaps well to mention in passing that Whitman's version of Emerson's static conception of unity (involving ideas of unity conceived in terms of singleness, simplicity, of balance, proportion, precision) is not, strictly speaking, static at all, since it derives from the identity of the artist and comes to his art organically by way of his expressing that identity. Whitman considered simplicity mainly in terms of the identity of "the full-sized man, unconquerable and simple"; but the simplicity of this full-sized man involved both candor and a kind of economy. With regard to simplicity conceived as candor Whitman had said that "all faults may be forgiven him who has perfect candor." He considered simplicity, conceived as candor, to be "the art of art, the glory of expression." "Nothing, " he said,

is better than simplicity—nothing can make up for excess, or for lack of definiteness. To carry on the heave of impulse and pierce intellectual depths and give all subjects their articulations, are powers neither common nor very uncommon. But to speak in literature with the perfect rectitude and insouciance of the movements of animals and the unimpeachableness of the sentiments of the trees in the woods and grass by the roadside, is the flawless triumph of art.[40]

Whitman would have the artist and his art be as simple and candid as objects in phenomenal nature.

Such candor involves as its corollary the denial of all ideas, of all ornaments brought to the work from outside—e.g., from irrelevant feudal and tribal traditions. Like Greenough, Whitman argued that "those ornaments can be allow'd that conform to the perfect facts of the open air, and that flow out of the nature of the work, and come irrepressibly from it, and are necessary to the completion of the work."[41] Like Thoreau he insisted that the "nature of the work, " including its ornamentation, derives initially and relates ultimately to the character, the identity of the artist as expresser. He argued that "the fluency and ornaments of the finest poems or music or orations or recitations are not independent [of the expresser] but dependent. All beauty, " he said, "comes from beautiful blood and a beautiful brain, "[42] i.e., from the identity of the expresser. "If the greatnesses are in conjunction in a man or woman it is enough." "The fact will prevail through the universe . . . but the gaggery and guilt of a million years will not prevail. Who troubles himself about his ornaments or fluency is lost."[43] "Words, " the media of fluency, the stuff of ornament in language, said Whitman, "follow character—nativity, independence, individuality."[44] To this may be added that not only the artist's words but the ideas he candidly expresses with them follow his character, his nativity, his individuality.

Whitman's insistence upon candor and economy, his insistence upon simplicity and directness of expression, may be
accountable in part to his lack of education in the formal rhet-
oric of ornament. It appears accountable in greater part, however, to his having accepted the Quaker's traditional pref-
erences: simplicity, lack of ornamentation, plain clothing,
plain speech, direct action. Candid expression as well as direct, economical action are the natural corollaries of the idea
of direct communion. The temperament that subscribes to one
is likely to subscribe to all—to deal as directly as possible with
the problems of knowing, saying, and doing. Whitman's "prudence" and Thoreau's "economy" represent, in a sense, versions of this mode of direct approach.

Whitman was not primarily concerned with unity conceived as
proportion or balance in the conventional rhetorical sense,
i.e., in terms of the physical arrangement of lines or locutions
on a page. He conceived of proportion, of balance, in terms of
that which in art is to be expressed: in his own art, of insights
into the facts of identity and the idea of identity. His work is
characterized, therefore, less by a lack of proportion, of balance or precision, than by his own particular versions of these
things. To Whitman proportion in art was achieved less by
physical arrangement than by the artist's insight into the matters of soul, of identity and the facts of identity—by his har-
monious expression of these in his art. Whitman believed that
beauty results from a candid expression of this special sense
of proportion. Such expression, he said,

is no chance of miss or hit—it is as inevitable as life—it is exact and
plumb as gravitation. From the eyesight [of the communicant] proceeds another eyesight, and from the hearing proceeds another hearing, and from the voice proceeds another voice, eternally curious of
the harmony of things with man. These understand the law of perfection in masses and floods. . . . This is the reason that about the
proper expression of beauty there is a precision and balance. [This is
the reason that] one part does not need to be thrust above another.[45]

Whitman's conception of balance does not rest, however, at
the level of mere equalitarian inclusiveness. It extends beyond
it, and involves a kind of Hegelian synthesis which characterizes both Whitman's art and his individual and general con-

ceptions of identity or soul. Indeed, Whitman's conception of democracy, insofar as it is ordered by these first two elements (the individual and the general) of his conception of soul appears to approximate the "Hegelian formula" as applied to "the categories of Essence." As G. R. G. Mure points out in referring to Hegel's thesis-antithesis-synthesis formula,

we shall find [regarding categories of essence, that] the relation of thesis to antithesis [is] that of identity to diversity, or of immediacy to mediation, rather than that of sheer affirmation to sheer negation. Here the synthesis will show identity in diversity, but in every triad the aspects of cancellation and preservation will be present together and almost in equipoise. [46]

Such is the relationship between the identity of self and of All in Whitman's conception of democracy. That Whitman was at least aware of the Hegelian formula, that he may have done serious reading in Hegel's logic, is suggested by his reference to it. [47] However, he may have developed independently his conceptions of soul, balance, and proportion, and merely noticed in passing the similarity between the German philosopher's line of reasoning and the results of his own communion with consciousness.

In any case Whitman's idea of balance, although apparently equalitarian, [48] involves the further idea of synthesis; and the particular kinds of inclusiveness characteristic of Whitman's verse are designed to serve that synthesis. Whitman was concerned with the synthesis of the one with the many, of the ideal with the real, in society and in his art. In society the synthesis of the one with the many (of self with All) was to be achieved by promulgating the idea of democracy. The synthesis of the ideal with the real (of the spiritual with the material) was to be achieved in the same way, by promulgating an ideal conception of identity which was more realistic than the current heroic conception deriving from feudal circumstances. Whitman believed that only a conception of identity which was consistent with the idea of the individual self, which was consistent with that "most spiritual and vaguest of earth's dreams, yet hardest of basic facts"—one capable of generalization without at the same time denying individual identities—was sufficiently realistic, as well as sufficiently ideal, for modern society.

Whitman's art was designed not only as an instrument to be

employed in achieving for society a synthesis of the one with
the many, of the real with the ideal, but it was designed also
as an exemplary demonstration of that kind of synthesis. A
synthesis of the real with the ideal, of the material with the
spiritual, was fundamental to the very kind of poetry that Whitman was writing. The material or real was involved in his concern with the facts of human experience, with his use of words
as things; the spiritual, or ideal, was involved in his concern
with vivifying these facts, not by means of imitation or by unusual arrangement, but by means of their consideration in
terms of his democratic conception of identity. Whitman at-
tempted to achieve in his art a synthesis of the self with All
by portraying the representative self as hero—by portraying
his own identity, his nativity, his connections with his phenomenal and social context—his containment of multitudes.

Whitman expressed this containment of multitudes in his
poetry indirectly through his copious use of nouns and lists of
nouns. These nouns are indirect to the extent that they are used
boldly, as dots of paint were used by Seurat, to suggest facts;
and they lead like the dots of paint, when viewed from the
proper point of view (i.e., one like Whitman's) to a kind of
agglomerative synthesis. By suggesting the identities of various
"Essential" categories of persons in America, e.g., teamsters,
carpenters, prostitutes, soldiers, savants, along with the facts,
the objects, and places common to their experiences—express
wagons, broadaxes, tenements, artillery pieces, books, Ore-
gons, Brooklyns, Dakotas, Paumanoks—Whitman presents
factually yet indirectly his idea of identity and the facts of that
identity, in short, his world picture. The over-all or cosmic
unity of Whitman's poetry derives accordingly from this world
picture. Hence Whitman's statement that his "poems when complete should be a *unity*, in the same sense that the earth is, or
that the human body (senses, soul, head, trunk, feet, blood,
viscera, man-root, eyes, hair), or that of a perfect musical
composition is."[49] Hence, the "great constituent elements of
[his] poetry . . . viz.: Materialism—Spirituality"[50]—and hence,
the difficulty of getting at Whitman's poetry by routes of approach deriving exclusively from knowledge of earlier poets
who subscribed to different conceptions of identity, and of
unity—to different views of art, of artists, and of the world.

The equalitarian, the inclusive, balance suggested by Whitman's particular use of nouns in his poetry does not show up
readily in its proper role, as leading to a cosmic unity or synthesis, unless it is viewed in terms of Whitman's world picture.
Unfortunately this final synthesis, this over-all or cosmic unity
which characterizes Whitman's art, does not become as clear
in *Leaves of Grass,* for example, as does a similar synthesis
in Eakins' portrait of Whitman, which is directed toward a
similar end. This is so in part because Whitman's canvas is
much larger and its draftsmanship more complex than Eakins',
because his work includes more facts, because it comes much
closer than Eakins' to standing in relation to all things. It is
so also because the mind does not synthesize the sensory effects of words as readily as the mind guided by the retina does
the effects of blobs of paint. These are two of the principal
reasons that the purport of Whitman's verse (its character, its
intention, its meaning) is more difficult to apprehend than that
of Eakins' work which is ordered by similar principles. The
third and most important reason that Whitman's purport is
difficult to see, that his conceptions of unity are difficult to
apprehend, is that his work is regularly studied in terms of
purports and conceptions of unity that are inapplicable to it.
His poetry will be obscure to some, argued Whitman, exactly
because of its purport—because it is addressed to the soul.
"Poetic style," he said, "when address'd to the soul is less
definite form, outline, sculpture, and becomes vista music,
half-tints, and even less than half-tints."[51] Whitman argued
that such obscurity was necessary to insure that his poetry
would be approachable only from the proper point of view.
Such poetry, he said, though aiming at completion, must be
forever incomplete until its readers have worked through its
demonstrations to an awareness of their own identities as seen
in Whitman's terms and in fulfillment of Whitman's purport.
"In fact," he said

a new theory of literary composition for imaginative works of the very
first class, and especially for higher poems, is the sole course open
to these States. Books are to be call'd for and supplied, on the assumption that the process of reading is not a half-sleep, but, in the
highest sense, an exercise, a gymnast's struggle; that the reader is
to do something for himself, must be on the alert, must himself or

herself construct indeed the poem, argument, history, metaphysical essay—the text furnishing the hints, the clue, the start or framework. Not the book needs so much to be complete but the reader of the book does. That were to make a nation of supple and athletic minds, well-train'd, intuitive, used to depend on themselves, and not on a few coteries of writers. [52]

"I seek less, " he concluded, "to state or display any theme or thought, and more to bring you, reader, into the atmosphere of the theme or thought—there to pursue your own flight"[53]—i.e., your own identity. Whitman's concern as literatus, as poet, as theologian, as representative American, was with the matter of identity (as self, as All), and its proper expression; and this matter of identity orders his ethics, his poetics, his esthetics; it orders his conceptions of unity, order, design. And this matter of identity, therefore, must condition any thoroughgoing critique of Whitman's art and his art theory. This is not to suggest that Whitman's conceptions of unity, of balance, of synthesis lead to anything exactly like the "system" suggested by Hegel's logic. However, it is to suggest that there is more design in Whitman's argument than he gets credit for.

NINE

WHITMAN

ON ARCHITECTURE

Like Emerson, Greenough, and Thoreau, Whitman was interested in other arts than his own; like them his interest focused
in part upon architecture. He believed that American architecture was as fit a subject for poetic treatment, as much representative of the facts and identity of America, as its rivers, its
teamsters, its savants. In his "Notes and Fragments," he
scribbled the suggestion for a "Poem of Architecture? The
Carpenter's and Mason's Poem,"[1] which he fulfilled in part
with his "Song of the Exposition," and his "Song of the Broad-
Axe."

What Whitman said about architecture supports, by giving
clear and simple examples, the purport he announced in his
poetics. Like Emerson he descended to lower ground in dis-
cussing architecture. As is natural to poets, he considered
language arts the highest: "To make a perfect composition in
words," he said, "is more than to make the best building or
machine, or the best statue, or picture—It shall be the glory of
the greatest master to make perfect compositions in words."[2]
In company with Emerson he considered painting and sculpture
declining in importance. "I am not sure," he said, "but the day
for conventional monuments, statues, memorials, &c., has
pass'd away—and that they are henceforth superfluous and
vulgar."[3] "It would seem painting, sculpture, and dramatic
theater . . . no longer play an indispensable or even important
part in the workings and mediumship of intellect, utility, or
even high esthetics."[4] But "architecture remains, doubtless
with capacities, and a real future. . . ."[5] Regarding the state

of current architecture, however, Whitman made some major reservations.

His criticism of American architecture was ordered by his ideas of simplicity, economy, and of prudence. Along with Emerson, Thoreau, and Greenough, he objected to the over-emphasis of the monumental or showy features of public archi-tecture—to the display in such architecture of the builder's or proprietor's concern with displaying wealth. Grace Church, he said, "is by superficial observers called beautiful. The proper word is not beautiful but showy."[6]

Grace Church inside and out is a showy piece of architecture, and the furnishing of the pews, the covering of the luxurious cushions, etc., appear to be unexceptionable, viewed with the eye of an upholsterer. The stainless marble, the columns, and curiously carved tracery, are so attractive that the unsophisticated ones of the congregation may well be pardoned if they pay more attention to the workmanship about them than to the preaching.[7]

"We don't see how," said Whitman, "it is possible for people to *worship God* there. It is a place where the world, and the world's traits, and the little petty passions and weaknesses of human nature, seem to be as broad blown and flush as upon the Exchange in Wall Street, Broadway, or any mart of trade, of a week day."[8]

Like Greenough, Whitman saw some evidence of mature at-tention in public architecture to its domestic- or useful-art functions. And like Greenough he saw also that American public architecture as a whole had a long way to go before it could ar-rive even at zero. "In Broadway," he said,

grand edifices have become so much a matter of course that what would ten years ago have caused the greatest admiration and comment, is now altogether *passé*. Some of the most magnificent stores in the world are now on Broadway—with still greater to come. With all these, among the elder buildings, only the Astor House, in its massive and simple elegance, stands as yet unsurpassed as a specimen of exqui-site design and perfect proportion. It is thoroughly modern in its uses and appropriateness to its purpose, but classic and severe as a Greek temple.[9]

Like Greenough, Whitman objected to the unconsidered bor-rowing of Greek forms without attention to Greek principles.

He observed that

> the Savings Bank in Bleeker street just east of Broadway is Grecian, of the most ornamental and florid order. It is a wonderful and lovely edifice. But the surroundings, (the Greeks always had reference to these,) are enough to spoil it—let alone the discordant idea of a Greek temple, (very likely to Venus) for a modern Savings Bank![10]

> Such considerations as these make one laugh at the architecture of the New York Custom House, with its white sides and its mighty fluted pillars. In the original some twenty-three or five hundred years ago, when Socrates wandered the streets of Athens talking with young men . . . there stood the original, the temple of the ideal goddess, the learned, brave, and chaste Minerva. It was of immense extent, and was manly, a simple roof supported by columns. There were performed the rites—in that city and among that people, they and the building belonged. And to that the United States government has gone back and brought down (a miniature of it,) to modern America in Wall street, amid these people these years, for a place to settle our finances and tariffs. How amusing![11]

Like Greenough, Whitman concluded that "at the present, few persons pay any attention to architecture in its higher planes, its philosophy, its reference to all other things, few have any profound idea of beauty in a building."[12] For he believed that true beauty, in building as in poetry, was the result of simple, candid expression of the facts and purports of the structure, of its site, its materials, its intended functions—the consideration of these ordered always by his conception of democracy. Thus, even as he was concerned with the nature of words as things, as the raw stuff of poetry representing by indirections the facts of American experience, Whitman was also concerned with the nature of building materials as the raw stuff of architectural expression, representing likewise the facts of American experience. Regarding the Crystal Palace, he commended the increasing use of iron and glass. He considered these materials more representative of the facts of modern society than feudal stone. "Iron and glass," he said, "are going to enter more largely into the composition of buildings. So far iron used in large edifices is a perfect success."[13] It is only a short step from Whitman's statement here to Frank Lloyd Wright's insistence upon the candid expression (i.e., respect) of the nature of materials in architecture.

In architecture as in poetry Whitman saw beauty resulting from proper expression achieved not only by attention to facts—to the materials and environs of the work, the facts of human identity—but by attention also to the efficient fulfillment of purports or functions. Like Greenough he saw the finest current expression of architectural functions, not in America's public architecture, but in its naval architecture. "The huge hull'd clean-shap'd New York Clipper," he said, "at sea under steam or full sail gleams with unmatched beauty."[14] More like Thoreau, however, he was concerned mainly with the domestic functions of architecture ashore. He insisted that domestic architecture ought to contribute to the realization of democracy. Like Thoreau he questioned the morality implicit in current standards of American dwelling-house architecture, particularly in large cities. Unlike Thoreau he did not suggest withdrawing from society to cabins in the woods; rather he proposed the construction in congested areas of tenement flats and in suburban areas of low cost housing.

Like Thoreau, Whitman charged that America's domestic architecture was too costly, and for that reason immoral. He blamed this condition upon the current preoccupation in America (in New York City at any rate) with the acquisition of wealth and with its ostentatious display. In a long newspaper article he objected to what he called "Wicked Architecture." Such architecture, he said, was

not wicked in carelessness of material construction, like the crumbly structures sometimes run up in our city by mercenary builders, that prove death-traps to the inmates; nor in purpose, like an Inquisition or a panel-thief's haunt; but in the uprighteous spirit of ostentation that unconsciously directs it, and in the manifold and frightful social evils following from it. [15]

"It may not at first appear," said Whitman,

that the architecture of New York has any very distinct connection with anything good or evil. But there *is* a connection, and one startlingly close and efficient. The domestic architecture—the dwelling house architecture—of the city (for our Architectural Wickedness exists mainly there), even though perhaps not absolutely in itself the efficient cause of evil, is the most striking type of that condition of

social morality which is the fertile hot-bed for evils the most enor-
mous.[16]

Whitman considered New York dwelling-house architecture
to be wicked because it did not provide adequately for the
proper functioning of the family of modest means. He considered a spacious, well-lighted, well-ventilated dwelling suitable for family living to be one of the three material prerequisites to the development of democracy. "A house to live in, " he
said, "is the third great necessity; food and clothing being before it." "Furthermore it is in some sense true that a man is
not a whole and complete man unless he owns a house and the
ground it stands on. . . . "[17]

Whitman believed accordingly that New York architecture
was wicked (i.e., inadequate to the realization of democracy)
because of the high cost of real estate and ostentatious treatment of it. "In New York, " he said, "closed in by rivers, pressing desperately toward the business center at its southern end,
and characterized by an unparalleled fierceness in money
chasing, land is dear. This of course makes the possession
of it a basis for an increased ostentation of it; for the dearer
a thing is, the more pride in showing it."[18] This building of
large, ostentatious dwellings by rich and ostentatious persons
would not lead to wicked consequences, argued Whitman, if it
were not for the fact that the "ways of thinking, throughout society are more or less formed on patterns set by the rich. "
The unfortunate consequence of these patterns of thought was
that "as a general principle . . . among all ranks except the
poorest, there is a habit of occupying houses outrageously and
absurdly too expensive, whether in prime cost or in rent, for
the resources of the occupant."[19] The wicked consequences
traceable directly to such a habit were those inherent in the
boarding house or rooming house existence caused by the need
of owners or renters of moderate means to sublet, and by the
need of families of even smaller means to rent cheap dwelling
space, however inadequate. The boarding house, argued Whitman, was a poor substitute for a home. He considered it "simply a place to keep a man's trunk and his wife while he is at
work, and where he had breakfast, tea, and sleeping room. "
"All day long, " he added, "these thousands and thousands of

wives, many of them with their children, are left alone, without responsibility, with little or no employment . . . they spin street yarns in Broadway; shop; dine at Taylor's or Thompson's; make calls; talk scandal; sleep. There is no chance for the gathering of the wretched husband's family.'[20]

By way of achieving a domestic architecture appropriate to the needs of the urban family in an emerging democracy, Whitman advanced two relatively simple plans. These he admitted were not to be considered long range solutions of the problem. "Of whatever remedies are applicable to this state of things," he wrote, "many are too profound and remote even to be stated in a newspaper article."[21] Yet by way of practical suggestion for immediate relief from some of the wickedness, he suggested for metropolitan areas in which property was expensive

the erection of tenement-houses, so arranged that each floor is a complete isolated habitation by itself. . . . Such tenements, judiciously located and handsomely furnished, could be rented at reasonable rates; would restore to many of the 'married bachelors' a place for their household goods, a home and hearth of their own . . . would furnish the unoccupied minds and listless bodies of their wives with the stimulus and responsibilities which they need, and which God meant for them: and last—and least—yet most necessary of all, could, as may be demonstrated, yield a remunerative percentage on the investment of the capitalist.[22]

Better still, as a means of eliminating the consequences of boarding-house living, Whitman suggested low-cost, suburban construction similar to that already appearing in Brooklyn. "Our architectural greatness," he said, consists not in the mansions of Manhattan, but "in the hundreds and thousands of superb private dwellings, for the comfort and luxury of the great body of middle class people—a kind of architecture unknown until comparatively late times, and no where known to such an extent as in Brooklyn. . . ."[23] He saw the validity of such a scheme of domestic architecture confirmed by the rapid growth of Brooklyn. "Perhaps the principal reason after all," he said, "of the unprecedented growth of Brooklyn in population is to be found in the fact that here men of moderate means may find homes at moderate rent, whereas in New York there 'is no medium' between a palatial mansion and a dilapidated hovel. . . ."[24]

In such a community as Brooklyn, "men of moderate means, living say at the rate of a thousand dollars a year or there-abouts," can live decently. "These men, comprising the most valuable class in any community . . . cannot afford to consume their salaries in paying house rent as they would inevitably be forced to do in New York if they wished to live in a respectable neighborhood. . . ."[25] "Property owners," concluded Whitman, "will, we think, find their account in erecting just such a class of buildings. There is a popular demand for them and nothing else will suit the people."[26] Voicing an effective popular demand for appropriate dwelling houses, rather than retreating to even more primitive living accommodations, as at Walden, was Whitman's recommendation for combating the general wicked-ness of American domestic architecture. Yet his attitude toward architecture was in the long run more like Thoreau's than, for example, Greenough's. Despite Whitman's concern with public architecture, despite his sympathetic interest in machinery, in building materials, the fact remains that he was more concerned with saving the soul (with the help of an appro-priate architecture) than he was with saving architecture per se. With respect to architecture at any rate, Whitman appears something like an urban, social, Quaker version of Thoreau.

TEN

CONCLUSION

Considered as estheticians only, apart from any examination of their art forms, Thoreau and Whitman are worth attending to because they have interesting and important things to say about some of the essential qualities of art and beauty. They have significant things to say about the nature of the artist and his responsibilities to himself and to his art—even as they have significant things to say about the artist's connections with his God, with nature, and with society.

These things continue to be intrinsically as well as historically significant because as writers Thoreau and Whitman were concerned as much with selecting appropriate strategies of thought as they were with chosing appropriate subject matter. As a consequence, in the process of explaining their theories they sometimes reveal not only unusual insights, but demonstrate significant modes of perspective—significant ways of achieving even further insights. Their writings are thus rich in suggestion. The things Thoreau and Whitman have to say on what amounts to esthetics continue relevant in our own time not only because these writers concerned themselves with matters of strategy and perspective in regarding subject matter, but also because neither one of them ever abandoned his basic assumption that a man's life itself must regulate the focus of his attention—whether that attention is directed upon art, or nature, or society, or salvation. And a man's life itself continues, even now, to be a topic of lively and relevant concern.

It is perhaps appropriate to say something at this point about the period in which this study of Thoreau and Whitman is being presented. It is a period which, from some viewpoints, appears to be marked by a reviving religious enthusiasm among intellectuals—many of whom are at the same time persons of a decidedly esthetic bent. It is perhaps for this very reason that Thoreau and Whitman are particularly instructive to us now: they suggest some valid relations between currently popular views of what can only be called religion (views similar to those entertained by these earlier writers) and the highly sophisticated art theories and art forms that surround our daily lives—and to which many of both the older and the newer versions of these religious views correspond. Indeed, even as Thoreau and Whitman have served us once in advancing from predominately religious considerations to predominately esthetic ones, they may now serve us again in suggesting the way back to establishing once more a desirable if not a necessary balance in our esthetic considerations between spiritual and formal concerns. It is just such a balance as this that these two writers never ceased to recommend—a balance, however, which we have not always chosen to consider important in our excitement with the prospect of applying particular materials and particular forms to our art.

We must never allow ourselves to forget, in this connection, that as estheticians Thoreau and Whitman were deeply concerned with salvation, and particularly with the role which art can play in contributing to it. It is important to remember, at the same time, that these writers concerned themselves with salvation in what amounts to a combination of both religious and secular (of both spiritual and worldly) senses. Thoreau, it will be remembered, was as deeply concerned as Cotton Mather ever was with the salvation of his soul, but unlike Mather he was concerned with saving his soul here, in this life, by way of living poetically the life of the true communicant in nature. Whitman, for his part, was concerned with salvation not only here, not only for himself as poet, not only for the individual democratic citizen, but for the whole nation, the entire hemisphere, the entire world, and, if possible, for all times to come.

Particularly in regarding Whitman's scheme of salvation, it is important to emphasize his concern with proposing an adequate art for democracy. Indeed, despite its difficult expres-

sion, we get from Whitman one of the best descriptions of that
spiritual democracy which is prerequisite to a healthy, lasting
democratic society (as well as to an appropriately democratic
art-expression) that has yet been uttered by a poet-theorist. As
a theorist Whitman advances a step beyond Thoreau's scheme
of salvation for the individual self, suggesting that salvation is
a social as well as a religious and an individual matter. In so
doing he posits, for one thing, a new democratic conception of
the heroic attitude. It is with reference to his crucial ideas of
the hero and of the attitude appropriate to the hero that Whitman is most commonly and perhaps most grievously misunderstood. This is so, in part, because Whitman, whether as poet
or as theorist, is a difficult writer. Particularly in regarding
Whitman's prose statements of his theory, readers have tended
to assume merely because the statements are difficult to understand—because they are full of high level abstractions often
left undefined—that these statements must necessarily be mean-
ingless. This simply is not so.

There is no denying that Whitman is a difficult writer, but
he is so for good and sufficient reasons. His theorizing is more
difficult than Thoreau's only in part because of the turgidity of
Whitman's prose. In many ways Whitman's ideas themselves
are more difficult than Thoreau's, partly because they are
more abstruse, partly because they are less familiar, and
partly because they are more comprehensive. Whitman not
only concerned himself, as did Thoreau, with living the individual life as poem, but he concerned himself also with such
matters as the nature of the ideal man's conception of self. He
was concerned with the ideal social and religious conditions,
with the ideal art and the ideal artists to produce such art, that
are necessary to the full realization and maintenance of his
scheme of salvation, which was more comprehensive than
Thoreau's—namely, with the realization of a truly democratic
society. In proposing to reform society rather than to escape
from its restrictions, Whitman took on a lot of responsibility,
and in his theory took on a large measure of difficulty, that
Thoreau avoided.

As has been suggested, Whitman tends both in his theory and
in his art forms to be more difficult than Thoreau partly because he is less conventional. The old learning can be applied

to Thoreau; he translates; his tropes are recognizable as such; he can be measured with conventional instruments—albeit such measurement requires both caution and wit. Whitman, as in stating his theory he tells us, has set out to be a poet that cannot be measured against a conventional scale; he posits a hero that is essentially unapproachable by way of conventional perspectives; his epic is not epic, his elegy is not elegiac in grossly conventional ways; his prosody, like his conception of the hero, is steadfastly nonfeudal, nonmedieval, insofar, indeed, as Whitman has been able to make it consistently so.

Although, as had been suggested, the esthetics of Thoreau and Whitman appear to be quite different, at least at the level of surface consideration, they have a great deal fundamentally in common. And it is precisely because they do have a great deal in common—despite differences in emphasis and scope—that these theories deserve to be studied together. Indeed, study of the one man's esthetic tends to inform study of the other's. Thus, even though Thoreau is more conventionally approachable as a theorist than Whitman, he is in some ways more radical in his attitudes. This is not the kind of thing a person is likely to discover without first comparing the two men's theories in considerable detail. By the same token, Thoreau's discussions regarding economy and the importance, practically, of achieving salvation here tend to inform Whitman's own discussions of the meanings he assigns to "prudence" and "soul."

Although the relations between Whitman's ideas and Emerson's have come to be taken pretty much for granted, similar kinds of relationships between Whitman's ideas and Thoreau's have not been given much attention. This book is designed to help fill in with some additional detail that larger scheme of relationships which it has been suggested do exist between the esthetic theories of those of our major writer-theorists who participated in what has been labeled the American Renaissance.

NOTES

Chapter One (pp. 3-9)

1. Henry David Thoreau, *Journal*, ed. Bradford Torrey (14 vols.; Boston: Houghton Mifflin Co., 1906), I, 240. The separately numbered *Journal* comprises volumes VII-XX of *The Writings of Henry David Thoreau*. Thus Vol. I of the *Journal* is Vol. VII of the *Writings*.

2. *Ibid.*, V, 4.

3. *Ibid.*, I, 464.

4. *Ibid.*, I, 51.

5. *Ibid.*, III, 157.

6. *Ibid.*, IX, 214.

7. Thoreau, *The Writings of Henry David Thoreau*, ed. Bradford Torrey (20 vols.; Boston: Houghton Mifflin Co., 1906), I, 310 *(A Week on the Concord and Merrimac Rivers)*.

8. *Journal*, IV, 126.

9. *Ibid.*, IV, 80.

10. *Writings*, II, 81 *(Walden)*.

11. *Ibid.*, VI, 213-14 *(Familiar Letters)*. My italics.

12. *Ibid.*, I, 310 *(A Week . . .)*.

13. *Ibid.*, II, 9 *(Walden)*.

14. *Ibid.*, II, 79.

15. *Ibid.*, II, 35.

16. *Journal*, III, 241.

17. *Writings*, II, 101 *(Walden)*.

18. *Journal*, V, 446.

19. *Writings*, II, 34 *(Walden)*.

20. *Ibid.*, II, 31.

21. *Ibid.*, II, 77.

22. *Ibid.*, II, 36.

23. *Ibid.*, II, 29.

24. *Ibid.*, II, 76-77.

25. *Ibid.*, II, 57.
26. *Journal*, III, 271-72.
27. *Ibid.*, II, 193.
28. *Ibid.*, I, 306.
29. *Writings*, II, 21 *(Walden).*
30. *Ibid.*
31. *Journal*, VII, 221.
32. *Writings*, VI, 161 *(Familiar Letters).*
33. *Journal*, V, 411.
34. *Ibid.*, V, 410.
35. *Ibid.*, V, 412.
36. *Journal*, IX, 246-47.
37. *Ibid.*, I, 368.
38. *Writings*, II, 16 *(Walden).*
39. *Ibid.*, II, 57.
40. *Writings*, VI, 259 *(Familiar Letters).*

Chapter Two (pp. 10-18)
1. Henry David Thoreau, *Journal*, ed. Bradford Torrey (14 vols.;
Boston: Houghton Mifflin Co., 1906), IV, 415.
2. *Ibid.*, IX, 205.
3. *Ibid.*, V, 506.
4. *Ibid.*, X, 252.
5. *Ibid.*, IX, 336.
6. *Ibid.*, IX, 209.
7. *Ibid.*, IX, 208.
8. *Ibid.*, X, 363-64.
9. *Ibid.*, VI, 294.
10. *Ibid.*, X, 127.
11. *Ibid.*, IV, 422.
12. Ralph Waldo Emerson, *The Journals of Ralph Waldo Emerson,
1820-1876,* ed. Edward Waldo Emerson and Waldo Emerson Forbes
(10 vols.; Boston: Houghton Mifflin Co., 1909-14), I, 313.
13. Thoreau, *The Writings of Henry David Thoreau,* ed. Bradford
Torrey (20 vols.; Boston: Houghton Mifflin Co., 1906), I, 350 *(A Week
on the Concord and Merrimac Rivers).*
14. *Ibid.*
15. Emerson, *Journals*, VI, 370-71.
16. Thoreau, *Journal*, VIII, 44.
17. Emerson, *Journals*, III, 474.
18. Thoreau, *Journal*, IV, 351.
19. *Ibid.*, V, 135.
20. *Ibid.*, XIII, 168-69.
21. *Ibid.*, IV, 174.
22. *Ibid.*, IV, 470.
23. *Ibid.*, V, 4.

24. *Ibid.*, XIV, 117.

25. *Ibid.*, XIII, 141.

26. *Ibid.*, X, 294.

27. *Ibid.*, XI, 285-86.

28. Lee Marten Nash, Ecology in the Writings of Henry David Thoreau, Master's thesis (No. 7065), University of Washington, 1951, p. 81.

29. *Journal*, III, 257.

30. *Ibid.*, III, 281.

31. Nash, Ecology in the Writings of Henry David Thoreau, p. 18.

32. *Journal*, XIV, 119.

33. *Ibid.*

34. Philip and Kathryn Whitford, in their article, "Thoreau: Pioneer Ecologist and Conservationist, " have concluded in this regard: "The lack of statistical analysis, which is the quality which a modern ecologist would criticize first, was a lack shared by all biological sciences in Thoreau's day. It is probably this lack that has caused Thoreau to be accepted slowly as a scientist, for, though his work was done before 1862, most of it was not known until the *Journals* were published in 1906, and by that time the concept of science had undergone the radical changes which brought increasing emphasis upon statistical analysis. . . ." *Scientific Monthly*, Vol. 73 (Nov., 1951), 291-96.

35. *Journal*, XII, 28.

36. *Ibid.*, X, 164-65.

37. *Ibid.*, IV, 236.

38. *Ibid.*

39. *Ibid.*

40. *Writings*, V, 131 *(Excursions and Poems)*.

41. *Ibid.*

42. *Journal*, IX, 490.

43. *Ibid.*, X, 69.

44. *Ibid.*, IX, 121.

Chapter Three (pp. 19-27)

1. Henry David Thoreau, *Journal*, ed. Bradford Torrey (14 vols. ; Boston: Houghton Mifflin Co., 1906), III, 401.

2. Ralph Waldo Emerson, *The Journals of Ralph Waldo Emerson, 1820-1876*, ed. Edward Waldo Emerson and Waldo Emerson Forbes (10 vols. ; Boston: Houghton Mifflin Co., 1909-14), IX, 546.

3. *Ibid.*, VI, 124.

4. Thoreau, *Journal*, III, 119.

5. Thoreau, *The Writings of Henry David Thoreau*, ed. Bradford Torrey (20 vols. ; Boston: Houghton Mifflin Co., 1906), I, 350 *(A Week on the Concord and Merrimac Rivers)*.

6. *Journal*, III, 99.

7. *Ibid.*, III, 368.

8. *Writings,* I, 363 *(A Week . . .).*

9. *Journal,* I, 328.

10. *Ibid.,* I, 450-51.

11. *Ibid.,* IV, 158.

12. *Ibid.*

13. *Ibid.,* IV, 239.

14. *Ibid.,* XI, 153.

15. *Ibid.,* III, 311.

16. *Ibid.,* II, 83.

17. *Ibid.,* III, 232.

18. *Ibid.,* X, 344.

19. *Writings,* I, 365 *(A Week . . .).*

20. *Journal,* II, 469.

21. *Writings,* I, 400 *(A Week . . .).*

22. F. O. Mathiessen, *American Renaissance* (New York: Oxford University Press, 1941), p. 133.

23. *Journal,* I, 240.

24. *Writings,* I, 365 *(A Week . . .).*

25. *Journal,* X, 239-40.

26. *Ibid.,* X, 159.

27. *Writings,* V, 125 ("Natural History of Massachusetts").

28. Charles R. Metzger, *Emerson and Greenough* (Berkeley and Los Angeles: University of California Press, 1954), pp. 39-43.

29. *Journal,* I, 92.

30. *Ibid.,* III, 324.

31. *Ibid.,* I, 360.

32. *Ibid.,* VII, 504.

33. *Ibid.,* I, 271.

34. *Ibid.,* V, 368.

35. *Ibid.,* VIII, 109-10.

36. *Ibid.,* XI, 37.

37. *Ibid.,* XI, 96.

38. *Ibid.,* V, 322.

39. *Ibid.,* VIII, 44-45.

40. *Ibid.,* XI, 285.

41. *Ibid.*

42. *Ibid.,* II, 166.

43. *Ibid.,* I, 145.

44. *Ibid.,* VI, 56.

45. *Ibid.,* I, 308.

46. *Ibid.,* X, 80.

47. *Ibid.,* I, 271.

48. *Ibid.,* I, 367-68.

49. *Ibid.,* I, 167.

50. *Ibid.*

51. *Ibid.,* I, 343.

52. *Ibid.*, I, 275.
53. *Ibid.*, XI, 296.
54. *Writings*, VI, 94 *(Familiar Letters)*.
55. *Journal*, I, 153. Compare this statement with the discussion of Whitman and Hegel, pp. 78-79.
56. *Ibid.*, V, 135.
57. *Ibid.*, IX, 121.

Chapter Four (pp. 28-38)
1. Henry David Thoreau, *Journal*, ed. Bradford Torrey (14 vols.; Boston: Houghton Mifflin Co., 1906), VIII, 464.
2. *Ibid.*, VII, 461.
3. *The Writings of Henry David Thoreau*, ed. Bradford Torrey (20 vols.; Boston: Houghton Mifflin Co., 1906), II, 64-65 *(Walden)*. Emerson had reported a similar sentiment of Greenough: "In the old Egyptian, and in the middle age architecture he [Greenough], sees only 'cost to the constituency,' prodigious toil of prostrate humanity." *The Journals of Ralph Waldo Emerson, 1820-1876*, ed. Edward Waldo Emerson and Waldo Emerson Forbes (19 vols.; Boston: Houghton Mifflin Co., 1909-14), VIII, 320.
4. Thoreau, *Journal*, IV, 153.
5. *Ibid.*, IV, 152.
6. Horatio Greenough, *Form and Function, Remarks on Art by Horatio Greenough*, ed. Harold A. Small (Berkeley and Los Angeles: University of California Press, 1947), pp. 20-21.
7. *Writings*, II, 51 *(Walden)*.
8. *Ibid.*
9. *Ibid.*, II, 39.
10. *Ibid.*, II, 37.
11. *Journal*, III, 240-41.
12. *Writings*, V, 100 *(Excursions)*.
13. *Ibid.*
14. *Writings*, IV, 28-29 *(Cape Cod)*.
15. *Ibid.*
16. *Journal*, I, 361.
17. F. O. Mathiessen, *American Renaissance* (New York, Oxford University Press, 1941), p. 153.
18. Greenough died December 18, 1852.
19. *Journal*, III, 181-83.
20. *Ibid.*, III, 183.
21. Greenough, *Form and Function*, pp. 60-61.
22. *Journal*, XI, 227.
23. Greenough, *Form and Function*, p. 59.
24. *Ibid.*
25. *Journal*, V, 525-26.
26. *Ibid.*, III, 183.
27. Greenough, *Form and Function*, p. 74.

28. Ibid., pp. 80-81.

29. *Ibid.*, p. 58.

30. *Ibid.*, p. 122.

31. *Ibid.*, pp. 80-81.

32. Both Thoreau and Greenough preceded Wright in their concern with the nature and functions of building materials: Greenough in complaining of the friable sandstone used in Washington, Thoreau in studying not only the habitat but the structural uses of trees. See also Whitman's references to cast iron and glass in his *An American Primer*, ed. Horace L. Traubel (Boston: Small, Maynard and Co., 1904), p. 8.

33. *Journal*, II, 278-79.

34. *Writings*, II, 74 *(Walden)*.

35. *Journal*, I, 367.

36. *Ibid.*, VI, 137.

37. *Writings*, II, 51-52 *(Walden)*.

38. *Ibid.*

39. *Ibid.*

40. Greenough, *Form and Function*, p. 71.

41. *Writings*, II, 51. A resolution of the conflict which Thoreau saw between his desire to improve the individual's life and Greenough's desire to improve architecture can be seen in Frank Lloyd Wright's assertion that good architecture can influence the life of the indweller as well as reflect it.

42. Ralph Waldo Emerson, "The Poet," *Essays by Ralph Waldo Emerson,* Second Series (Boston: Houghton Mifflin Co., 1903), p. 37.

Chapter Five (pp. 39-46)

1. Walt Whitman, *The Complete Writings of Walt Whitman*, ed. Richard Maurice Bucke, Thomas B. Harned, and Horace L. Traubel (Paumanok Edition, 10 vols.; New York: G. P. Putnam's Sons, 1902), V, 270 *(Prose Works*, II, "Notes Left Over"). The separately numbered *Prose Works* comprises volumes IV-X of *The Complete Writings of Walt Whitman*. Thus Vol. II of the *Prose Works* is Vol. V of *The Complete Writings*.

2. *Ibid.*, V, 265.

3. That Whitman was profoundly influenced by Pietist religious thought is suggested by the references in his prose writings to his maternal grandmother's being a Quaker, to his mention of being taken as a child by his father to hear Elias Hicks preach, by his several references to George Fox and to Hicks (especially the thirty pages of notes for a proposed biography of Hicks), *Complete Writings*, Vol. VI, as well as the employment in his poetry of Quaker ideas and terminology: e.g., the "Idea of God being male and female" (see Emory Holloway, "Walt Whitman and the Shakers," *Colophon,* February, 1933) and his "constant use of Quaker terminology, such as First Day, Fifth Month, and other forms of plain and direct speech of historic Quakerism" (see Howard W. Hintz,

"The Quakerism of Walt Whitman, "*Modern American Vistas* [New York: The Dryden Press, 1940], p. 456).

4. Emerson had observed, for example, that "the Unitarian preacher who sees that his Orthodox hearer may with reason complain that the preaching is not serious, is by that admission judged. . . . But when a man speaks from deeper convictions than any party faith, when he declares the simple truth, he finds his relation to the Calvinist or Methodist or Infidel at once changed in the most agreeable manner. He is of their faith, says each. It is really a spiritual power which stopped the mouths of the regular priests in the presence of the fervent First Quaker and his friends. If the dead-alive never learned it before that they do not speak with authority from the highest, they learn it then, when a commissioned man comes, who speaks because he cannot hold back the message that is in his heart." *The Journals of Ralph Waldo Emerson, 1820-1876,* ed. Edward Waldo Emerson and Waldo Emerson Forbes (10 vols.; Boston: Houghton Mifflin Co., 1909-14), I, 313.

5. *Writings,* V, 191 ("Collect").

6. *Ibid.,* V, 182 ("Preface of 1855 to *Leaves of Grass"*).

7. *Ibid.,* IX, 151.

8. *Ibid.,* IV, 183 ("Specimen Days").

9. "It seems indeed, " wrote Whitman, "as if peace and nutriment from heaven subtly filter into me as I slowly hobble down these country lanes and across fields, in the good air—as I sit here in solitude with Nature—open, voiceless, mystic, far removed yet palpable eloquent Nature. I merge myself into the scene, in the perfect day. "*Ibid.,*IV, 182.

10. Ralph Waldo Emerson, *The Complete Works of Ralph Waldo Emerson,* ed. Edward Waldo Emerson (Concord Edition, 12 vols.; Boston: Houghton Mifflin Co., *ca.* 1903-21), I, 335.

11. *Writings,* VI, 259-61 ("November Boughs").

12. *Ibid.,* V, 133-34.

13. Of metaphysics Whitman announced: "The culmination and fruit of literary artistic expression, and its final field of pleasure for the human soul, are in metaphysics, including the mysteries of the spiritual world, the soul itself, and the question of the immortal continuation of identity." *Ibid.,* V, 136 n. ("Democratic Vistas").

14. Of Nature, however, Whitman was careful to assert in superaddition to his concept of soul: "As by what we now partially call Nature is intended at most, only what is entertainable by the physical conscience, the sense of matter, and of good animal health—on these it must be distinctly accumulated, incorporated, that man, comprehending these, has, in towering superaddition, the moral and spiritual consciences. . . ." *Ibid.,* V, 135.

15. *Ibid.,* IV, 307.

16. *Ibid.,* V, 104.

17. *Ibid.,* VI, 259.

18. *Ibid.*, VI, 261.

19. *Ibid.*, V, 281.

20. *Ibid.*, V, 174.

21. *Ibid.*, V, 105.

22. *Ibid.*, V, 104-5.

23. *Ibid.*, V, 105. My italics.

24. Whitman's derivation of insight as well as sanction from communion with soul ranks him as a communicant on a level with Emerson and Greenough, who got insight as principle deriving from communion with nature, and with Thoreau, who got it as ecological perspective deriving also from nature.

25. *Writings*, V, 140. My italics.

26. *Ibid.*, V, 77.

27. *Ibid.*, V, 132-33. My italics.

28. *Ibid.*, V, 131.

Chapter Six (pp. 47-56)

1. Walt Whitman, *The Complete Writings of Walt Whitman*, ed. Richard Maurice Bucke, Thomas B. Harned, and Horace L. Traubel (Paumanok Edition, 10 vols.; New York: G. P. Putnam's Sons, 1902), V, 43 *(Prose Works,* II, "Specimen Days"). "The question of Nature, largely considered, " added Whitman, "involves the question of the esthetic, the emotional, and the religious—and involves happiness. A fitly born and bred race, growing up in right conditions of out-door as much as in-door harmony, activity and development, would probably from and in these conditions, find it enough merely to *live*—and would in their relations to the sky, air, water, trees, &c., discover and achieve happiness." *Ibid.*, V, 134 ("Collect").

2. "Not Nature alone is great, " he said, "in her fields of freedom and the open air, in her storms . . . the mountains, forests, seas—but in the artificial, the work of man too is equally great—in the profusion of teeming humanity—in these ingenuities, streets, goods, houses, ships. . . ." *Ibid.*, V, 64.

3. *Ibid.*, V, 287.

4. *Ibid.*, V, 49.

5. *Ibid.*, V, 297.

6. *Ibid.*

7. *Ibid.*, V, 125.

8. *Ibid.*, V, 68.

9. *Ibid.*, V, 77.

10. *Ibid.*, V, 69-70. In this sense, said Whitman, the spiritual idea of "Democracy too is law, and of the strictest, amplest kind . . . it is the superior law, not alone that of physical force, the body, which, adding to, it supersedes with that of the spirit. Law is the unshakable order of the universe forever; and the law over all, the law of laws, is the law of successions; that the superior law [i.e., democracy], in time,

gradually supplanting and overwhelming the inferior one." *Ibid.*, V, 79.

11. *Ibid.*, V, 102.

12. *Ibid.*, V, 97.

13. *Ibid.*, V, 80.

14. *Ibid.*, V, 69.

15. *Ibid.*, V, 112-13.

16. H. S. Canby, an exception, states in his article, "Thoreau and Whitman in Democracy, " that "Thoreau was a spiritual economist, Whitman a spiritual sociologist. . . . When it came to the progress of American society in the years before the Civil War, in which material and moral issues were inextricably mingled, both men had their feet solidly on the ground." *The Saturday Review of Literature,* Vol. XXIV, No. 8, July 19, 1941.

17. *Writings,* V, 99.

18. *Ibid.*, V, 285.

19. *Ibid.*, V, 61.

20. *Ibid.*, V, 143.

21. *Ibid.*, V, 63.

22. *Ibid.*, V, 99-100.

23. *Ibid.*, V, 124-26.

24. *Ibid.*, V, 100.

25. *Ibid.*

26. *Ibid.*, V, 99.

27. *Ibid.*, V, 100.

28. *Ibid.*, V, 72.

29. *Ibid.*, V, 112.

30. *Ibid.*, V, 101.

31. *Ibid.*

32. *Ibid,*, V, 111.

33. *Ibid.*, V, 148-49.

34. *Ibid.*, V, 123.

35. *Ibid.*, V, 137.

36. *Ibid.*, V, 123-24.

37. *Ibid.*, V, 58.

38. *Ibid.*, V, 51.

39. *Ibid.*, V, 53.

40. *Ibid.*

41. *Ibid.*, V, 130.

42. *Ibid.*, V, 96.

43. "I submit, " said Whitman, "that the fruition of democracy, on aught like a grand scale, resides altogether in the future." *Ibid.*, V, 92.

44. *Ibid.*, V, 59.

45. *Ibid.*, V, 288.

46. *Ibid.*, V, 202.

47. *Ibid.*, V, 53-54.

48. *Ibid.*, V, 54.

Chapter Seven (pp. 57-65)

1. Cf. the following with Whitman's reference to Carlyle on page 57: "I was at first roused to much anger and abuse by this essay 'Shooting Niagara' from Mr. Carlyle, so insulting to the theory of America—but happening to think afterwards how I had more than once been in the like mood, during which his essay was evidently cast, and seen persons and things in the same light . . . I have since read it again, not only as a study, expressing as it does certain judgments from the highest feudal point of view, but have read it with respect as coming from an earnest soul, and as contributing certain sharp-cutting metallic grains, which, if not gold or silver, may be good, hard, honest iron." Walt Whitman, *The Complete Writings of Walt Whitman*, ed. Richard Maurice Bucke, Thomas B. Harned, and Horace L. Traubel (Paumanok Edition, 10 vols.; New York: G. P. Putnam's Sons, 1902), V, 71 n.

2. *Ibid.*, V, 163.

3. *Ibid.*, V, 175.

4. *Ibid.*

5. *Ibid.*, V, 81.

6. *Ibid.*, V, 175.

7. *Ibid.*, V, 167.

8. *Ibid.*, V, 98.

9. *Ibid.*, IX, 9.

10. *Ibid.*

11. *Ibid.*, V, 132.

12. *Ibid.*, VII, 9.

13. *Ibid.*, V, 202.

14. Thus, of Darwin Whitman said: "The world of erudition, both moral and physical, cannot but be eventually better'd and broaden'd in its speculations, from the advent of Darwinism. Nevertheless, the problem of origins, human and other, is not the least whit nearer its solution." *Ibid.*, V, 279.

15. *Ibid.*, V, 190.

16. *Ibid.* The extent to which Whitman entered into science is suggested by Mrs. Alice Lovelace Cooke's article, "Whitman's Indebtedness to the Scientific Thought of His Day," *The University of Texas Bulletin*, Studies in English, No. 14, July, 1934, pp. 86-115.

17. *Writings*, V, 99.

18. "He who does great deeds," said Whitman, "does them from his innate sensitiveness to moral beauty.—all great rebels and innovators, exhibit the highest phase of the artistic spirit. The painter, sculptor, the poet, express heroic beauty better in description; but the others are heroic beauty, the best belov'd of art." *Ibid.*, VI, 88.

19. *Ibid.*, V, 171.

20. *Ibid.*, IX, 30.

21. "Judah lives," said Whitman, "and Greece immortal lives, in a couple of poems." *Ibid.*, V, 55.

22. *Ibid.*, V, 55-56.
23. *Ibid.*, V, 56.
24. *Ibid.*, V, 55.
25. *Ibid.*, V, 89.
26. *Ibid.*, V, 218.
27. *Ibid.*, V, 217.
28. *Ibid.*, V, 177.
29. *Ibid.*, V, 164-65.
30. *Ibid.*, V, 172.
31. *Ibid.*, V, 164.
32. *Ibid.*, V, 172-73.
33. *Ibid.*, V, 169.
34. *Ibid.*, V, 178-79.
35. *Ibid.*, V, 180.
36. *Ibid.* Even as Thoreau, Whitman saw the life of the prudent man as poem: "Love the earth and sun and the animals, despise riches, give alms to every one that asks, stand up for the stupid and crazy, devote your income and labor to others, hate tyrants, argue not concerning God, have patience and indulgence toward the people, take off your hat to nothing known or unknown, or to any man or number of men . . . re-examine all you have been told in school or church or in any book, and dismiss whatever insults your own soul; and your very flesh shall be a great poem, and have the richest fluency, not only in its words, but in the silent lines of its lips and face, and between the lashes of your eyes, and in every motion and joint of your body." *Ibid.*, V, 166.
37. *Ibid.*, V, 169.
38. "Has any one fancied," said Whitman, that "he could sit at last under some due authority, and rest satisfied with explanations, and re-alize, and be content and full? To no such terminus does the greatest poet bring—he brings neither cessation nor shelter'd fatness and ease. The touch of him, like Nature, tells in action." *Ibid.*, V, 182.
39. *Ibid.*, V, 170.
40. *Ibid.*, IX, 10.
41. *Ibid.*, V, 222.
42. *Ibid.*, V, 165-66.
43. *Ibid.*, V, 165.
44. *Ibid.*, V, 216.
45. *Ibid.*, VI, 279.
46. *Ibid.*, IV, 307.
47. *Ibid.*, V, 171.
48. *Ibid.*, V, 169.

Chapter Eight (pp. 66-82)
1. Walt Whitman, *With Walt Whitman in Camden*, Vol. I, ed. Horace L. Traubel (Boston: Small, Maynard and Co., 1906), 100.
2. Whitman, *The Complete Writings of Walt Whitman*, ed. Richard

Maurice Bucke, Thomas B. Harned, and Horace L. Traubel (Paumanok Edition, 10 vols.: G. P. Putnam's Sons, 1902), III, 64.

3. *Ibid.*, IX, 10.

4. Whitman, *Leaves of Grass*, ed. Emory Holloway (New York: Doubleday and Company, 1948.), p. 373.

5. *Writings*, V, 139.

6. Whitman, *With Walt Whitman in Camden*, Vol. II, ed. Horace L. Traubel (New York: D. Appleton and Co., 1908), 26.

7. *Writings*, III, 46. "A perfect user of words, " said Whitman, "uses things. . . ." Whitman, *An American Primer*, ed. Horace L. Traubel (Boston: Small, Maynard and Co., 1904), p. 14.

8. *Writings*, V, 138.

9. *Ibid.*, V, 138-39.

10. *Ibid.*, V, 177.

11. Cf. Professor Matthiessen's discussion, *American Renaissance* (New York: Oxford University Press, 1941), p. 606.

12. *Writings*, V, 98.

13. *Ibid.*, III, 45-46.

14. *Ibid.*, V, 66.

15. Whitman, *With Walt Whitman in Camden*, Vol. IV, ed. Sculley Bradley (Philadelphia: University of Pennsylvania Press, 1953), 121.

16. *Ibid.*

17. *Ibid.*, IV, 4.

18. *Writings*, V, 139.

19. *Ibid.*, V, 218.

20. *Ibid.*, V, 139.

21. *Ibid.*, III, 65.

22. *Ibid.*, III, 47.

23. These six passages are located in Whitman's works as follows: *Writings*, V, 135, "high literary and esthetic composition"; *Ibid.*, V, 138, "the poet, the esthetic worker in any field"; *Ibid.*, V, 288, "the sane, eternal moral and spiritual-esthetic attributes"; *An American Primer*, p. 34, "Names are a test of the esthetic and of spirituality"; *Writings*, V, 205, "esthetik worthy the present condition"; *Ibid.*, III, 65, denial of his poetic performance "as aiming mainly toward art or aestheticism."

24. *A New English Dictionary*, ed. Sir James Augustus Murray (20 vols.; Oxford: The Clarendon Press, 1888-1929).

25. *Writings*, V, 138.

26. *Ibid.*, V, 288.

27. *Ibid.*, V, 205. My italics. That others beside Whitman were concerned with the term *esthetic* is suggested by Elizabeth Palmer Peabody's article on "The Word 'Aesthetic'" in the single issue of her *Aesthetic Papers* (Boston: The Editor, 1849), p. 4. She observed at the end of her article that "the word aesthetic is difficult of definition, because it is the watchword of a whole revolution in criticism. Like Whig and Tory, it is the standard of a party; it marks the progress of an idea.

It is as a watchword we use it, to designate, in our department, that
phase of human progress which subordinates the individual to the general, that he may re-appear on a higher plan[e] of individuality."

28. *A New English Dictionary.*

29. *Writings*, V, 170.

30. *Ibid.*, V, 177.

31. *Ibid.*, V, 203.

32. *Ibid.*, IX, 3.

33. *Ibid.*, III, 54.

34. *Ibid.*, III, 65.

35. *Ibid.*, V, 203. My italics.

36. *Ibid.*, V, 126. My italics.

37. "Song of the Answerer, " *Leaves of Grass,* p. 143.

38. *Writings,* V, 203.

39. *Ibid.*, V, 166.

40. *Ibid.*, V, 170. Note the various opposite meanings of the word
simple: it can mean stupid or candid, crude or efficient, primitive or
urbane.

41. *Writings*, V, 177.

42. *Ibid.*, V, 166.

43. *Ibid.*

44. *An American Primer*, p. 2.

45. *Writings*, V, 168.

46. G. R. G. Mure, *An Introduction to Hegel* (Oxford: The Clarendon
Press, 1940), p. 136.

47. *Writings*, V, 141.

48. "Did you suppose, " said Whitman, "there could only be one Supreme? We affirm that there can be unnumbered Supremes; and that
one does not countervail another any more than one eyesight counter-
vails another. . . ." *Writings*, V, 172.

49. *Ibid.*, IX, 3.

50. *Ibid.*

51. *Ibid.*, V, 202.

52. *Ibid.*, V, 148.

53. *Ibid.*, III, 58.

Chapter Nine (pp. 83-89)

1. Walt Whitman, *The Complete Writings of Walt Whitman,* ed.
Richard Maurice Bucke, Thomas B. Harned, and Horace L. Traubel
(Paumanok Edition; New York: G. P. Putnam's Sons, 1902), X, 24.

2. Whitman, *An American Primer,* ed. Horace L. Traubel (Boston;
Small, Maynard and Co., 1904), p. 28.

3. *Writings*, V, 295.

4. *Ibid.*, V, 57.

5. *Ibid.*

6. Whitman, *The Gathering of the Forces,* ed. Cleveland Rodgers and

John Black (New York: G. P. Putnam's Sons, 1902), II, 94.

7. *Ibid.*, II, 91.

8. *Ibid.*, II, 95.

9. Whitman, *I Sit and Look Out,* ed. Emory Holloway and Vernolian Schwartz (New York: Columbia University Press, 1932), p. 128.

10. *Ibid.*

11. *Ibid.*, p. 129.

12. *Ibid.*

13. *Ibid.* Speaking with reference to the uses of new architectural materials as bearing even upon the words, the materials of poetry, Whitman announced: "If iron architecture comes in vogue, as it seems to be coming, words are wanted to stand for all about iron architecture . . . those blocks of buildings, seven stories high, with light strong facades, and girders that will not crumble a mite in a thousand years." *An American Primer,* p. 8.

14. *Writings,* V, 176.

15. Whitman, "Wicked Architecture," *Walt Whitman, Complete Poetry and Selected Prose and Letters,* ed. Emory Holloway (New York: Columbia University Press, 1938), p. 607.

16. *Ibid.*

17. *Ibid.*

18. *Ibid.*

19. *Ibid.*, p. 608.

20. *Ibid.*, p. 611.

21. *Ibid.*, p. 612.

22. *Ibid.*

23. Whitman, *Uncollected Poetry and Prose of Walt Whitman,* ed. Emory Holloway (New York: Columbia University Press, 1921), II, 253.

24. *I Sit and Look Out,* p. 145.

25. *Ibid.*

26. *Ibid.*

BIBLIOGRAPHY

Canby, Henry Seidel. "Thoreau and Whitman on Democracy, " *The Saturday Review of Literature*, 24:8, July 19, 1941.

Cooke, Alice Lovelace. "Whitman's Indebtedness to the Scientific Thought of His Day, " *The University of Texas Bulletin*, Studies in English, No. 14, July, 1934, pp. 86-115.

Emerson, Ralph Waldo. *The Complete Works of Ralph Waldo Emerson*, ed. Edward Waldo Emerson. 12 vols. Concord Edition. Boston: Houghton Mifflin Co., *ca.* 1903-21.

—————. *Essays by Ralph Waldo Emerson*, Second Series. Boston: Houghton Mifflin Co., 1903.

—————. *The Journals of Ralph Waldo Emerson, 1820-1876*, ed. Edward Waldo Emerson and Waldo Emerson Forbes. 10 vols. Boston: Houghton Mifflin Co., 1909-14.

—————. *Nature Addresses and Lectures by Ralph Waldo Emerson*, ed. Edward Waldo Emerson. Boston: Houghton Mifflin Co., 1930.

—————. *Ralph Waldo Emerson: Representative Selections*, ed. Frederic I. Carpenter. New York: American Book Company, 1934.

Greenough, Horatio. *Form and Function, Remarks on Art by Horatio Greenough*, ed. Harold A. Small. Berkeley and Los Angeles: University of California Press, 1947.

Harding, Walter Roy. *A Thoreau Handbook*. New York: New York University Press, 1959.

Hintz, Howard, Grebanier Hintz, and D. N. Bernard, eds. *Modern American Vistas*. New York: The Dryden Press, 1940.

Holloway, Emory. "Walt Whitman and the Shakers, " *Colophon*, February, 1933.

Matthiessen, F. O. *American Renaissance*. New York: Oxford University Press, 1941.

Metzger, Charles R. *Emerson and Greenough*. Berkeley and Los Angeles: University of California Press, 1954.

Mure, G. R. G. *An Introduction to Hegel.* Oxford: The Clarendon Press, 1940.

Nash, Lee Marten. Ecology in the Writings of Henry David Thoreau. Master's thesis, No. 7065, University of Washington, 1951.

Peabody, Elizabeth Palmer, ed. *Aesthetic Papers.* Boston: The Editor, 1849.

Thoreau, Henry David. *Correspondence,* ed. Walter Harding and Carl Bode. New York: New York University Press, 1958.

—————. *The Writings of Henry David Thoreau,* ed. Bradford Torrey. 20 vols. *Journal,* vols. 7-20. Boston: Houghton Mifflin Co., 1906.

Whitford, Philip and Kathryn. "Thoreau: Pioneer Ecologist and Conservationist, " *Scientific Monthly,* Vol. 73, Nov., 1951, pp. 291-96.

Whitman, Walt. *An American Primer,* ed. Horace L. Traubel. Boston: Small, Maynard and Co., 1904.

—————. *The Complete Writings of Walt Whitman,* ed. Richard Maurice Bucke, Thomas B. Harned, and Horace L. Traubel. 10 vols. Paumanok Edition. New York: G. P. Putnam's Sons, 1902.

—————. *The Gathering of the Forces,* ed. Cleveland Rodgers and John Black. Vol. II. New York: G. P. Putnam's Sons, 1920.

—————. *I Sit and Look Out,* ed. Emory Holloway and Vernolian Schwartz. New York: Columbia University Press, 1932.

—————. *Leaves of Grass,* ed. Emory Holloway. New York: Doubleday and Company, 1948.

—————. *Uncollected Poetry and Prose of Walt Whitman,* ed. Emory Holloway. New York: Columbia University Press, 1921.

—————. *Walt Whitman: Complete Poetry and Selected Prose and Letters,* ed. Emory Holloway. London: The Nonesuch Press, 1938.

—————. *With Walt Whitman in Camden,* ed. Horace Traubel. Vol. 1, Boston: Small, Maynard and Co., 1906. Vol. 2, New York: D. Appleton and Co., 1908. Vol. 3, New York: Mitchell Kennerly, 1914.

—————. *With Walt Whitman in Camden,* ed. Sculley Bradley. Vol. 4, Philadelphia: University of Pennsylvania Press, 1953.

INDEX

111